MAGNA CARTA LOOPHOLE
GULLIBLE TAXPAYER LAW

A Review of Canadian Bank Law Section 165(3)
Tort of Conversion and the Collecting Bank

This volume is personal account of tax deductible securities fraud not disproved in court. Crawford has made every effort to simplify financial matters that readers may review the 2017 Supreme Court of Canada decision to deny trial for COMER – Committee on Monetary and Economic Reform Class Action for clarification of bank law. The work refers to Pitman's Bills, Cheques, and Notes, and Thomson's Dictionary of Banking eBook material available to read from the Internet.

Published by New Generation Publishing in 2019
Copyright © Anthony Crawford 2019
Edited by Jill Crawford
Cover art by David Lowe

The author asserts the moral right under the Copyright, Designs and Patents Act 1988 to be identified as the author of this work.

All Rights reserved. No part of this publication may be reproduced, stored in a retrieval system or transmitted, in any form or by any means without the prior consent of the author, nor be otherwise circulated in any form of binding or cover other than that which it is published and without a similar condition being imposed on the subsequent purchaser.

ISBN: 978-1-78955-858-6

www.newgeneration-publishing.com

This volume is a second edition of written works and PowerPoint presentation since 2002 that disclaimers still apply as specified in Original Material available on request.

Narrative Refs: CBC, Legal Transcripts, TVCogeco Your Vote 2006, and US Syndicate CoasttocoastAM

References:
1. Magna Carta Principle. 2. Tax Law. 3. Real Estate Tax Shelter Schemes.
4. Income Tax Credit Savings. 5. Tax Scams for the Rich. 6. Bank System. 7. System Analysis. 8. Securities Fraud. 9. Legalese. 10. Budget Process.

Title: Magna Carta Loophole Gullible Taxpayer Law.
Subtitle: Double Presentment.

Canadian Law Section 165(3) Scholarly Review

The Tort of Conversion and the Collecting Bank

Margaret H. Ogilvie, Chancellor's Professor Carlton University, Ottawa, Canada, reviewed section 165(3);

"[People] have despaired of courts restoring sense to this area of the law and have expressed the hope that Parliament will intervene to amend the BEA along the lines of other common law countries. But legislation to protect banks is likely to be politically too unpopular for any government to act, so that it seems more sensible to appeal to the courts to review the law. Plentiful resources exist in scholarly literature, which is unanimous on the changes required to restore fairness and sanity to these not infrequent cases. But for the fact that these cases of employee defalcation involve cheques, the banks would never be involved and the loss would lie with the responsible parties.

Yet, it would be relatively simple for the courts to do what is required to restore fairness– in particular, to re-visit their interpretation of sections 20(5) and 165(3) and follow the lead of other common law courts in re-visiting the question of defences in the tort of conversion.

This is, after all, how the common law has evolved naturally over the centuries!

Hopefully, the courts have not been entirely seduced by the spirit of the present age that it is always someone else's fault."

I took a system approach to study the bank effect of improperly earned income tax credits hidden from the Treasury not reported in the budget and I recommend a transaction control number for transparent account.

Section 165(3) Cheque Delivery Process Analysis

Ten-Step Bank Transaction *'Off-site Loans Closings'*

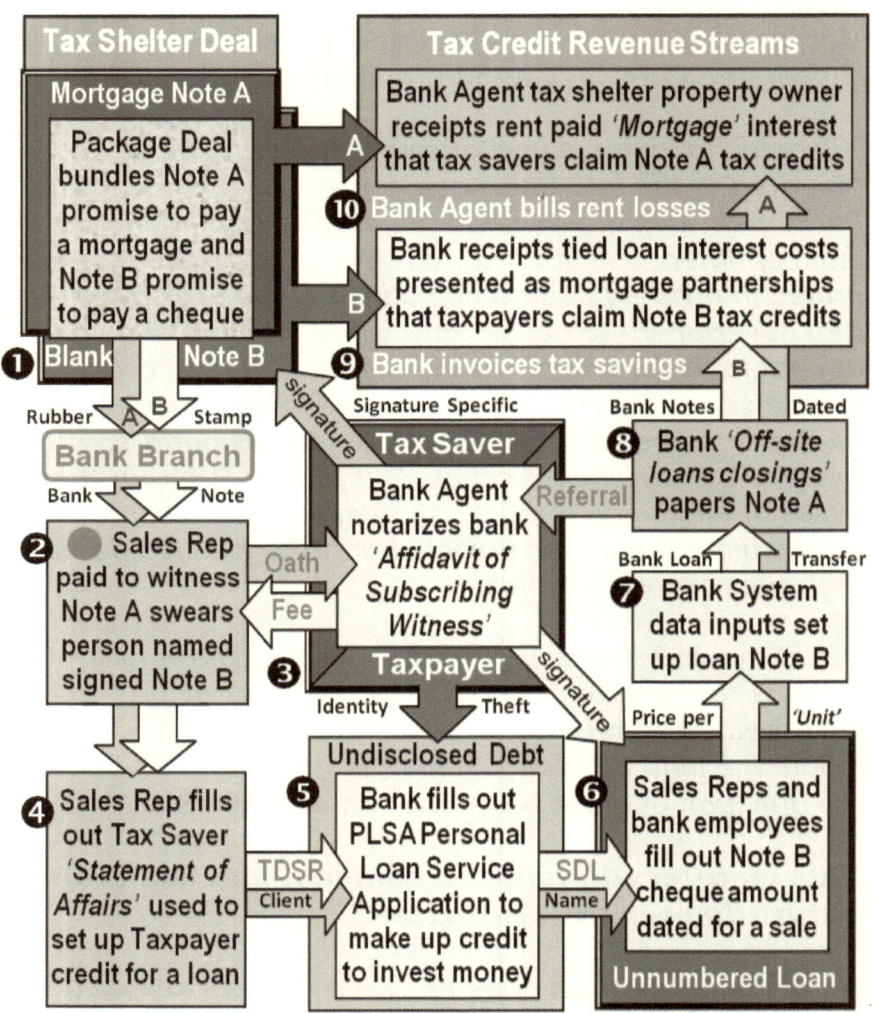

This research refers to 2009 ABCP *'Crisis in Canada'* report from Prof John Chant, Simon Fraser University of the $32b largest bankruptcy of a financial conduit in Canadian history. Workflow and cash flow analysis retraces Rent Seeking Tax Arbitrage through the ABCP *'Acquire-to-Distribute'* business model in the report.

Section 165(3) Cheque Conversion Cash Flow

Ten to Thirteen-Step Transaction Tax Credit Windbill Cash Flow

Double Presentment Twice Paid Tax Credit Windbill Interest

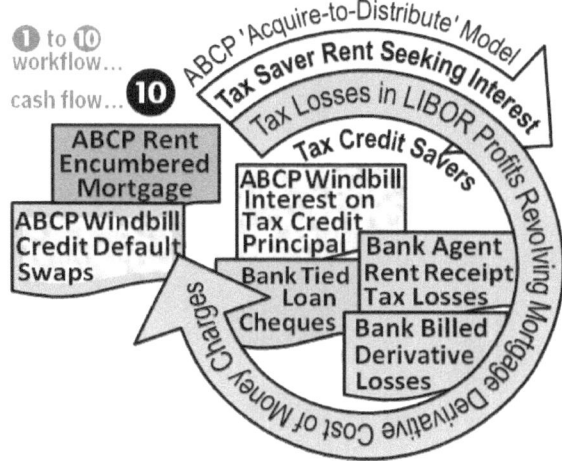

Double Presentment Twice Paid Tax Credit Windbill Principal

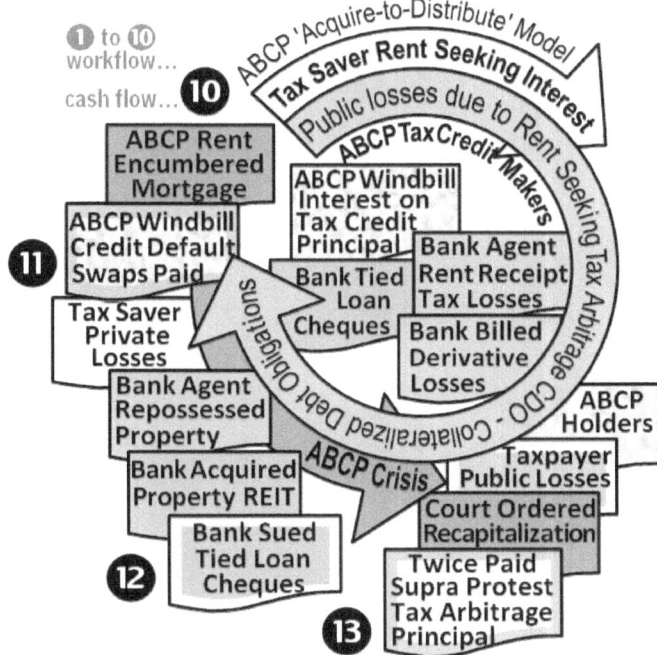

CRAWFORD'S MAGNA CARTA LOOPHOLE GULLIBLE TAXPAYER LAW

This is a review of Canadian Section 165(3);

Where a cheque is delivered to a bank for deposit to the credit of a person and the bank credits him with the amount of the cheque, the bank acquires all the rights and powers of a holder in due course of the cheque...

Which in the case of Rent Seeking Tax Arbitrage...

Any taxpayer can sign a promise to repay money for a private imaginary dollar as a tax-credit saver Windbill *'Maker'* that a conversion through the Treasury coins a public notional national debt real dollar to its *'Holder'* in due course.

Material References
Legal definitions from Black's Law, words defined from Webster' Dictionary, bank terms from Thomson's Dictionary of Banking, Windbill principle from Pitman's Bills, Cheques, and Notes, with other definitions of banking terms as noted in page footnotes.

USURISM TERMINOLOGY [1]

Glossary of Terms	
Acronym	**Meaning**
ABCP	Asset Backed Commercial Paper
BBC	British Broadcasting Corporation
BIS	Bank of International Settlements
BoE	Bank of England
CBC	Canada Broadcasting Corporation
CCAP	Central Computer Accreditation Process
CDS	Credit Default Swap
CDO	Collateralized Debt Obligation
COMER	Committee on Monetary Economic Reform
CRA	Canada Revenue Agency
DPA	Deferred Prosecution Agreement
FBI	Federal Bureau of Investigations
FSA	Financial Services Authority
ICB	Independent Commission on Banking
IEITC	Improperly Earned Income Tax Credit
ICAO	Institute of Chartered Accountants Ontario
IMF	International Monetary Fund
INET	Institute for New Economic Thinking
IPERA	Improper Payments Elimination and Recovery Act
IRS	Internal Revenue Service
LIBOR	London Inter-Bank Offered Rate
MP	Member of Parliament
MPP	Member of Provincial Parliament
PLSA	Personal Loan Service Application
PM	Prime Minister
SDL	Sitting Duck Loan after namesake debtor
SIV	Structured Investment Vehicle
TIGTA	Treasury Inspector General for Tax Administration

---

[1] USURISM *The doctrine that moneymaking is the highest good and that moral duty is fulfilled through usury.* Ref: Urbane Dictionary. http://www.urbandictionary.com/define.php?term=Usurism&defid=6740771

**Capitalism Without Capital
Canadian Tax Deductible Snow Jobs**

MAGNA CARTA LOOPHOLE
GULLIBLE TAXPAYER LAW

TABLE OF CONTENTS

1. Tax Credit Billionaire President Trump 11
2. Bank of England 1694 Omnibus Bill 15
3. Storybook Sleazy Tax Shelter Schemes 19
4. True Dough Loonies and Toonies 23
5. Canadian Tax Deductible Snow Jobs 25
6. Committee on Monetary and Economic Reform 31
7. Ruly English Words of Law to Command 35
8. The Bank is Always Right Rule 39
9. Wisdom of Lawmakers is no Concern of the Law 47
10. Court Ordered Debt in Justice 59
11. Signature-Specific Identity Theft 63
12. Light Touch Bank Regulation 69
13. Never Sign a Windbill Rule 75
14. Front and Back Office Windbill Sales 81
15. Twice Paid Tax Credit Windbill Posters 87
16. Don Quixote Tilts at Windbills 95
17. Capitalism without Capital Ponzi 105
18. Constitutional Class Action Lawsuit 117
19. Comer Motions to Consider in Appeal 133
20. COMER 2017 Ruling in Review 141
21. Will the Last Person Standing Please Sit Down 149
22. Private and Public Regrets 157
23. Twice Paid Tax Credit Windbill Deficit Dollars 161
24. Consumer Safeguards and Taxpayer Protection 167
25. Magna Carta Loophole Gullible Taxpayer Law 171
26. Taxpayer Signed Letters of Credit 179
27. Crawford Submission to the 2017 Tax Plan 191
28. Magna Carta Loophole ABCNotes of Law 205

1. Tax Credit Billionaire President Trump

Billion dollar tax scams for the rich are impossible to imagine and hard to believe except in Ways and Means of Magna Carta Loophole Gullible Taxpayer Law.

The first tax-credit millionaire was probably Dutch born William III King of England who monetized the tax-credit worth of the English in the Bank of England tally of the first deficit economy in the world in 1694.

Magna Carta Loophole Gullible Taxpayer Law was composed in Ruly English in the Bills of Exchange Act, 1882. It was found in the Federal Court of Canada in 2015, which I reported to the Finance Committee in 2017.

Real-estate tax-credit billionaire Donald Trump was elected the richest 45th President of America in 2017.

Americans voted the prospect of a billionaire candidate President of Corporate America. It was a new image of independence in politics. The media followed Trump in all he did and said, and wherever he went. They said he knew more about making a deal than anyone else.

Donald Trump was elected because of knowing social media better than anyone, *"I understand social media. I understand the power of Twitter. I understand the power of Facebook maybe better than almost anybody, based on my results, right?"* he said in November 2015.

And campaign contributions, *"I used to be, George, the fair-haired boy— you know, when I was a contributor. I know more about contributions than anybody,"* he confirmed in November 2015.

That was how he worked the social media to win the election, according to Trump. That and *'America First'*.

Especially jobs, *"I hope all workers demand that their teamsters endorse Donald J. Trump. Nobody knows jobs like I do! Don't let them sell you out!"* he broadcast in January, 2016.

And of course, banking, *"Nobody knows banking better than I do,"* he bragged in February 2016.

And politicians, *"Nobody knows politicians better than Donald Trump,"* he said at a rally in February 2016.

And trade, *"Nobody knows more about trade than me,"* he told people in March 2016.

And Wall Street, an NBC interviewer asked Trump, *"You're a guy who said you know the Wall Street bankers better than anyone?" "Better than anyone,"* said Trump in April 2016.

"I think nobody knows more about taxes than I do, maybe in the history of the world. Nobody knows more about taxes," Trump reassured people in May 2016. And income; *"Nobody knows more about taxes than I do, and income than I do,"* again in May. And as the king of debt, *"Nobody knows more about debt. I'm like the king. I love debt,"* was also reported in May 2016.

It was all about his money, *"I understand money better than anybody. I understand it far better than Hillary, and I'm way up on the economy when it comes to questions on the economy,"* he said later in June 2016.

And the establishment, *"I am a person that used to be establishment when I'd give them hundreds of thousands of dollars. But when I decided to run, I became very antiestablishment, because I understand the system better than anybody else,"* was how Trump explained money in politics in July 2016.

And systems of government, *"I think nobody knows the system better than I do,"* he said it again in August 2016.

And tax law, *"I understand tax laws better than almost anyone"* he said. And, *"I know our complex tax laws better than anyone who has ever run for president and am the only one who can fix them,"* on the Internet in October 2016.

And taxation, *"Donald Trump slams the U.S. tax code as 'unfair,' but he vows to use his own understanding of it to fix it for Americans,"* the media announced to taxpayers everywhere. They all followed the campaign.

He was fearlessly contentious and always controversial.

Donald Trump was so divisive on so many issues that several Republican Party members were opposed to his candidacy. They rallied for a more traditional politician in the Federal race for the White House.

Democrat, Hilary Clinton raised public interest in tax in the November 2016 US President Candidate debate, *"He hasn't paid any Federal income tax."* she accused Trump, *"That's because I'm smart,"* he quipped.

Trump had a mindset for tax reform, he called himself king of debt, he profited by it, and he claimed to know more about taxation better than anyone in history, *"I understand tax laws better than almost anyone, which is why I'm the one who can truly fix them."*

People believed in Trump as he promised to reform tax that they voted for him, and he won with a landslide.

US President Trump is the most famous perhaps most infamous tax-credit billionaire and Democrats doubted his wealth that they want to see his tax returns.

Trump must know more about making money before tax— than taxpayers who pay for his tax-credit dollars.

Whatever people think of US President Trump and his real estate deals in tax returns, there's a lesson from the master of tax-owed debt is money. If nothing else, people should stop to listen, and pause to think.

Trump is a tax credit billionaire on account of debt.

Because if a tax-deficit dollar isn't money he'd be poor.

In May 2019, Morgan Management and Aurora Capital Advisors were charged with conspiracy to commit half a billion dollar mortgage fraud around 2007 to 2017. It was reported that defendants inflated property value in off-the-book accounting how banking institutions and government-sponsored Freddie Mac and Fannie Mae issued more in debt than secured in real estate.

Wire Fraud in the US carries some 30 years in prison.

US Treasury Inspector General for Tax Administration, called TIGTA estimated some US$150billion tax scams behind IEITC – Improperly Earned Income Tax Credits. And, the IPERA – Improper Payments Elimination and Recovery Act, 2010 was passed to reclaim falsehoods.

President Trump spoke about fraud, and said it better than anyone on January 27, 2017 at the White House in his Inaugural Address;
~~~~~~~~~~~
"The wealth of our middleclass has been ripped from their homes and distributed all across the world. But, that is behind us and we are looking only to the future."
~~~~~~~~~~~

2. Bank of England 1694 Omnibus Bill

Middleclass struggled for rights and freedoms started in 1215 Magna Carta behind Civil War that a Republic of England ended monarchial rule in 1648. It moved all powers of Crown and Throne to lawmakers in the government order of a Bench that sat in Parliament.

The English returned to constitutional monarchy when George Sevile Halifax withdrew his support for James II, in the 1680s. He was in favor of William of Orange who had married Mary daughter of the Duke of York. Parliament invited foreign invasion that a Dutch King and English Queen came to rule England in 1689.

A *'Convention Parliament'* declared James II abdicated in the Bill of Rights Act, which gave the Crown to both King William III and Queen Mary II to rule in 1689.

The Act eliminated Divine Right of Kings and abolished successive Royals that Parliament ruled supreme in all decisions in a limited constitution of monarchial powers. Royals could no longer decree law, or suspend law, nor increase tax, or raise an army in peace time.

The Act founded free speech in Parliament and the right to petition the Crown. The Bill excluded James II and all heirs and Roman Catholics from the throne. And William swore to maintain the Protestant religion in the coronation rites of ascension.

Around 1691, a Scottish financier, William Patterson advised the government to create a Bank of England to manage national affairs in the Treasury Account. The plan was agreed and Charles Montagu Halifax floated a government account of national debt in 1692 behind the creation of the Bank of England in 1694.

The Bank of England Charter was an omnibus bill in the *'Tonnage Act'* how the government banked public wealth in a private bank that printed national debt on banknotes billed as currency for the interest cost of rent to use *'Bills of Exchange'* as money in the first deficit economic system in the world, in 1694.

An Omnibus Bill contains codependent provisions that its executive must sign in full acceptance, or veto the main provision of the Act within the Act.

Their Majesties, William and Mary signed Royal Assent in law to raise £1,200,000 plus £300,000 in annuities by subscription and incorporation in firm style of the, *'Governor and Company of the Bank of England'*;

'An Act for granting to their Majesties several duties upon tonnage of ships and vessels, and upon beer, ale, and other liquors, for securing certain recompenses and advantages in the said Act mentioned, to such persons as shall voluntarily advance the sum of fifteen hundred thousand pounds towards carrying on the war with France.'

The Act created a financial revolution that required the reinvention of cash flow in all its Ways and Means.

New English money, which used to tally to total credit worth of Treasury issued tax receipts for taxes paid, changed to Dutch money that Bank of England printed banknotes to the total loaned value of unpaid taxes on account of government debt borrowed from future tax owed to report and return through the bank system.

Prior to the Bank of England the Royals collected tax to fund war until it was paid on credit of national debt on account of £1.2m in 1694, reached £12m in 1700, rising to £850m in 1815 in Napoleonic Wars.

It was the start of national and international banking and beginning of capitalistic views that people elected representatives to define the law to make money, tax wages and earnings of commercial enterprise, and to budget how to pre-distribute tax in the best interest of citizens in a socioeconomic system for common good.

Governments promote democratic values in capitalism that socialism came to divide left from right leanings in politics. Politicians narrowed their sights on power to control people, while bankers expanded theirs on tax-billed moneymaking and ever increasing debt to profit.

The Bills of Exchange Act, 1882 established bank law that aside from amending Acts, money rules of law are much the same as the Charter for the Tonnage Act.

World War I cost £650m in 1914 reached £7.4b debt in 1919, and climbed to £24.7b through World War II.

Banks enjoyed the benefit of private interest on public debt for 250 years until Bank of England stock was acquired into public ownership after World War II that the Bank of England Act, 1694 was amended in 1946.

In centuries of lawmaking for moneymaking since the creation of the Bank of England the unequal outcome is seriously flawed that the wealth of the rich overtook the welfare needs of the poor across capitalism— at the furthest ends of a divided society than ever before.

In 2014, Oxfam reported from a Swiss mountain resort of Davos World Economic Forum, attended by the richest *'Global Elite'*, expressed concern that as few as 85 superrich have as much money as the poorest half of humankind. A paper entitled, *'Working For The Few'* shows only 1% own nearly 50% of all of global wealth.

The doctrine that private citizens vote representatives into public office to tax bad behavior out of society, and incent what they want ruled in— is not working.

The 1694 reformation of money transformed its governance in the form of a three-in-one *'triune-system';*

'...an orderly, interconnected complex arrangement of parts, a set of principles linked to form a coherent doctrine, a method of organization, administration or procedure'

Canada has a reputation for decency and fair play that Magna Carta Loophole Gullible Taxpayer Law for the rich was challenged in court pleading that the justice system should help tackle tax avoidance and evasion, especially in case of criminal banking.

~~~~~~~~~~~

3. Storybook Sleazy Tax Shelter Schemes

In 1997, the IRS – Internal Revenue Service referred TIC – Tax Innovation Center products to the FBI – Federal Bureau of Investigations, and a few years later the US Senate reviewed tax shelter schemes;

'...by 2003, dubious tax shelter sales were no longer the province of shady, fly-by-night companies with limited resources. They had become big business, assigned to talented professionals at the top of their fields and able to draw upon the vast resources and reputation of the country's largest accounting firms, law firms, investment advisory firms, and banks.'

The Subcommittee on Investigations criticized ethical standards of the legal and accounting profession. They said it pushed, prodded, bent, and sometimes broke the law for enormous monetary gain. In 2005, it forced KPMG to make a public apology for creating so-called;

'Storybook sleazy tax shelter schemes'.

The IRS and FBI were also concerned about the long-term effects in world economies. In 2005, the Senate Permanent Subcommittee on Investigations described the abusive intent of tax shelter schemes;

'...transactions in which a significant purpose is the avoidance or evasion of federal, state or local tax in a manner not intended by the law.'

Mortgage fraud cases doubled in the USA since 2006 to 1,800 in 2008. The FBI said it had reached such a level that rather than pursuing individual purchasers, it focused on professionals behind the most fraudulent schemes with the greatest impact on the US economy.

In February 2009, the FBI broadened its scope to 500 investigations of fraud citing 38 major companies directly connected to the financial crisis. The Deputy Director told the Senate Judiciary Committee, *"...it is a matter of lawyers, brokers, or real estate professionals systematically trying to defraud the system."*

When financial seizure was reported in August 2007 it was first assessed in $billions and then $trillions. The cause of the problem was generally put down to lack of regulation and unsecured bad debt. Especially, owed to subprime mortgages and overextended loans called CDO's – Collateralized Debt Obligations, widely held as if assets, but actually rigged to dilute and spread financial risk around the world. TIC included; subprime mortgages, ABS – Asset Backed Securities, SIV's – Structured Investment Vehicles, and ABCP – Asset Backed Commercial Paper Third Party Notes.

In December 2007, the New York Times described the problem as, *'Innovating our Way into Financial Crisis'*;

'The innovations of recent years – the alphabet soup of CDO's and SIV's, RMBS and ABCP's were sold on false pretenses. They were promoted as ways to spread risk, making investments safer. What they did instead— aside from making their creators lots of money, which they didn't have to repay when it all went bust— was to spread confusion, luring investors into taking on more risk than they realized.'

In February 2008, German HVB Group paid $29.6m to avoid indictment for defrauding the IRS and several KPMG executives faced charges in the largest criminal tax evasion scheme in US history. The IRS predicted $<u>billion</u> fines against law firms, accounting firms, and banks, for *'abusive'* tax shelter schemes;

'...each of these products generated hundreds of millions of dollars in phony paper losses for taxpayers, using a series of complex, orchestrated transactions, structured finance, and investments with little or no profit potential,' the US Subcommittee filed a report.

In March 2008, the IMF – International Monitory Fund measured sub-prime mortgage component about 20% compared to 80% bank losses due to ABS, CDO and SIV at some trillion dollar losses in world economies.

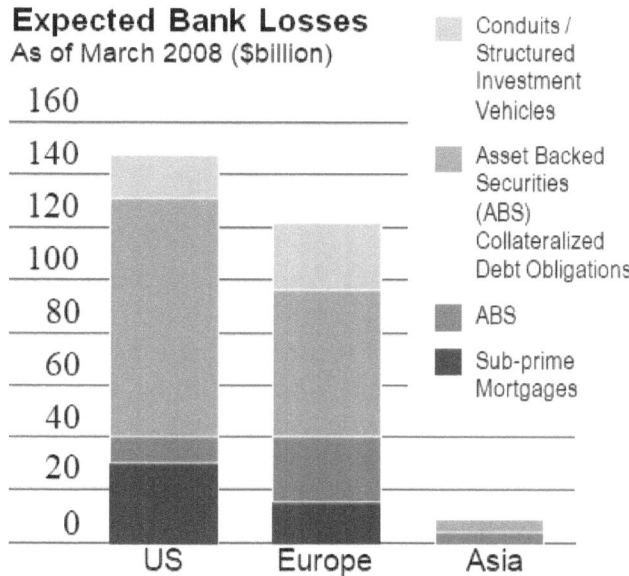

Sources: Reinhart and Rogoff This Time is Different (NBER 2008) IMF

In Canada, seizure in global markets resulted in the largest $32b bankruptcy protection of a financial conduit in Canadian history. Near $117b losses were ascribed to $32b Non-bank Notes, and some $85b due to Bank Notes. The government set up a Pan Canadian Committee to settle complaints from financial institutions, and about 1800 retail investors.

Canadian banks refused to absorb Non-bank Notes in 2009, and the government agreed to arrange a bailout for banks wanting immunity from prosecution.

ABCP settlement was defined in the Montreal Accord.

This was my experience in Canada. The same as the FBI and US Subcommittee on Investigations described the subprime mortgages crisis due to lawyers, brokers, and real estate dealers coining counterfeit tax-credit dollars through banking, geared to defraud by design.

There was no doubt people suffered a global crisis. There was no confusion the Bank of England Governor blamed the banking system. And there was no misunderstanding that all the big chiefs of all main banks denied any knowledge of any causal effect behind the Global Credit Crunch.

Wall Street bankers defended their institutions before the FCIC – Financial Crisis Inquiry Commission in 2010. But, CEOs were mostly reported for flippancy than financial judgment. Especially, Lloyd Blankfien, Chief Executive, Goldman Sachs who astonished the world when he testified he was, *"Doing God's Work"*.

He didn't actually say which God.

The complexity of banking was such a mystery in the media, and academia, that religion came into the fold to bridge the widening gap of unknown unknowns.

Canada gave me the best possible education in justice to prototype a socioeconomic system that worked on the language of law to operate. I read *'Notes of Law'* a lawyer left in a prayer book that gave me all the words any scholar of money could ever want.

~~~~~~~~~~~

4. True Dough Loonies and Toonies

Donald Trump was not the only political leader elected to reform tax; Justin Trudeau also promised to reduce tax in his campaign for Canadian Prime Minister in 2015, a year before Trump for US President, in 2016.

Trudeau was elected in 2016 and Trump in 2017 when income tax changed in Canada and America as tax fairness was an election promise in both countries.

Prime Minister Justin Trudeau described tax scams for the rich when he spoke at the United Nations in 2017,

"We raised taxes on the wealthiest one per cent so that we could lower them for the middleclass and we're continuing to look for ways to make our tax system more fair. We have a system that encourages wealthy Canadians to use private corporations to pay a lower tax rate than middleclass Canadians. That's not fair, and we're going to fix it..."

Finance Minister, Bill Morneau was also on television speaking about the inequity of tax in Canada. He said it was a system problem to be rid of loopholes that he hoped the public would help with good advice,

"The systems we are talking about are currently legal. We see though, that the implications of these structures create an unequal playing field. So, we don't think that they're fair. What we are really doing is closing down loopholes."

"The consultation paper looks at tax planning using private corporations in detail and sets out some potential policy responses. We want to hear from Canadians about how these polices would affect them, where we have it right and where we can improve."

The Prime Minister had his own view when he said,

"The budget will balance itself."

So, the Finance Department heard from taxpayers, but listening and hearing are two different things.

Indeed 100 year old taxpayer, William Krehm sued the government alleged in breach of Constitutional Law with respect to Magna Carta principle especially the *'No taxation without representation'* clause.

Rocco Galati, constitutional lawyer for William Krehm filed Action in the name of a *'Think Tank'*, COMER – Committee on Monetary and Economic Reform, Krehm founded in Toronto in the 1980s.

The COMER lawsuit became famous in Canada in the news that the Crown objected to trial claiming it was a misuse of courts especially that a political issue is not judiciable— that it should never be tried in court.

I was asked to testify as an expert witness in computer design with respect to a bank system failure behind Magna Carta Loophole Gullible Taxpayer Law as it may coin twice-paid tax-credit Windbill deficit dollars.

Prime Minister Brian Mulroney replaced the one dollar bill with a Canadian dollar coin called a *'Loonie'* in 1987, and Prime Minister Jean Chrétien doubled the loonie called a *'Toonie'* in bimetal mint in 1996.

~~~~~~~~~~~

5. Canadian Tax Deductible Snow Jobs

To some, Canada is the go to place for making sense fake money where fraud is up, arrests are down, and white-collar crime is just another snow job.

The ICAO – Institute of Chartered Accountants Ontario followed a complaint about an accountant in 2006 as it charged a CA - Chartered Accountant of wrongdoing;

'THAT, the said Michael G. Perris, in or about the period February 9, 1989 through December 31, 2001, while engaged in the practice of public accounting, referred a client or clients to products or services of others, and directly or indirectly accepted a commission or other compensation for that referral, contrary to Rule 216 of the rules of professional conduct.'

The governing body fined its unruly CA $5,000.

Perris had been countersued by a client and the CRA – Canada Revenue Agency intervened in the case; how works of art donated to charities for tax credits must be receipted for purchase cost— rather than appraised value. When judgment ruled Perris breached fiduciary duty for having received a secret commission selling a tax-scam deal, it established precedent law in 2004.

The Revenue Agency closed a tax-credit loophole from the sentence against Perris, but it didn't stop there...

Canadians generally blamed the Global Credit Crunch on US Subprime Mortgages in default that triggered debt around the world. The government commissioned Prof John Chant of Simon Fraser University, BC, to study ABCP – Asset Backed Commercial Paper in the $117b market failure and largest $32b bankruptcy of a financial conduit in Canadian history in 2008.

Prof Chant defined a 2009 ABCP *'Acquire-to-Distribute'* business model of nontraditional off-the-book banking including ABCP bank roles and procedures. It billed loans to invoice tax-credit deposits in off-the-balance-sheet shadow banking, which is not regulated. The report endorsed the Montreal Accord that recapitalized so-called toxic loans, and it recommended education for sales reps to better understand the ABCP market.

I was interested to study the ABCP *'Crisis in Canada'* Report with fraud in mind of the Canadian experience of the ABCP *'Acquire-to-Distribute'* business model how Perris was involved in tax deductible snow jobs.

It helped I had IBM Canada experience on structured system methodology with Chuck Morris at IBM Raleigh that we had launched JAD – Joint Application Design in Toronto in 1989. I wrote a book that Prentice Hall published *'Advancing Business Concepts in a JAD Workshop Setting'* in 1994. It had good reviews and the Committee on Finance invited me on a study of budget policy that involved public input in the 1st Session of the 35th Parliament in 1994.

Chairperson, Jim Peterson, directed a government goal to reduce the deficit by 3% of GDP – Gross Domestic Product, and my submission was on Page 51 Issue 72; 'CONFRONTING CANADA'S DEFICIT CRISIS', I said,

"As far as the deficit is concerned, I do believe it is a major problem. I find that the principles of fiscal management have eroded over the years. And, I would question the very nature of the business practices we implement in this country, which challenge the wealth-creation concept. I believe, from a personal point of view, that my wealth has been confiscated. I have a lot of friends who feel the same way."

After my experience in Committee on Finance meetings for then Prime Minister, Hon Paul Martin, I became an advocate for a more transparent banking. It was later I met Minister of Finance, James Flaherty, in November 2008 when we spoke about bank law and practice how lenders paid for signatures to setup loans that moved retail savings into tax scam pockets for the rich.

The minister promised to criminalize *'Identity-Theft'*. But he died, and it's still an issue today. And, NDP – New Democratic Party, leader, Hon Jack Layton signed a Private Members Bill to change the law.

On February 27, 2009 NDP MPP Andrea Horwath read *'Signature-Specific-Identity-Theft'* Petition 44 to reopen an OSC – Ontario Securities Commission investigation into trick-bank-loan dependent tax shelter schemes.

The WSJ – Wall Street Journal launched a G20 Future of Finance Initiative that I joined the 2009 convening as a Canadian delegate. It was there I met Gary Cohn, President Goldman Sachs Group, and we spoke about the phenomena of casino banking trick loans.

The WJS quoted his view, which was the same as mine,

'I do not think that commercial banks should take retail deposits that they're empowered to collect and need to protect... and lend them into high-risk capital markets. There should be segregation of the retail deposit base and capital-markets activity,' reporting Gary Cohn.

One hundred delegates defined G20 priorities and we discussed most crucial bank reforms with Professor Larry Summers, Director, National Economic Council, in a meeting room at the White House, where my own concern about identity theft was rephrased to become a requirement, which was voted the highest priority;

'Stronger Underwriting Standards ~ Bank Management and bank examiners must enforce the bank's minimum underwriting standards, focused on borrowers' ability to repay debt from income. Enforce supervisors' authority beyond banks to mortgage brokers and other bank agents. Ensure national real estate appraisals.'

The 2009 Future of Finance Initiative was featured in WSJ news that focused on problems and solutions the same as the 2009 ABCP *'Crisis in Canada'* Report.

The main concern in Canada was ABCP eligibilities that ABCP investment products were unregulated and with no distinction that banking was either on-, or off-bankbooks. Prof Chant labeled each bank function in his ABCP *'Acquire-to-Distribute'* business model;

ABCP 'Conduits' held assets in 'Trust' that issued debt 'like' money, 'Sponsors' construed 'Conduits' to sell commercial paper, 'Asset Providers' supplied debt processed through conduits, 'Distribution Agents' sold conduit value to 'Equity Investors' also 'Liquidity Providers' liable to repay mortgages in default of 'Credit Events' called 'Market Disruptions'.

Minister of Finance, James Flaherty, announced the report; *'A Research Study Prepared for the Expert Panel on Securities Regulation,'* subtitle, *'The Implications for the Regulation of Financial Markets'*, in the news;

'We are taking an important first step toward a new regulatory regime.'

The minister was quoted in Canadian national news,

'Yesterday Federal Finance Minister Jim Flaherty encouraged critics to read the panel's report with an open mind.'

"...To think about the need for consumer protection to think about what has been happening in the world and to take a Canadian approach."

The news broadcaster ended the newsbyte;

'In the meantime Flaherty doesn't want to say whether he expects that approach to include a court fight.'

But a fight over tax had already begun.

A centenarian Canadian taxpayer pushed tax reform on the world stage with a constitutional challenge that lawyer Rocco Galati for the founder of the COMER, *'Think Tank'*, William Krehm, and friend and respected member, Ann Emmett.

COMER alleged that when Prime Minister Pierre Elliot Trudeau changed monetary policy to use foreign bank loans to borrow money from offshore to print Canadian money onshore— Canada paid near two trillion dollars more for currency from 1974 than before, since 1933.

Galati pled the case in the Federal Court of Canada in 2015 for trial that William Krehm and Ann Emmett sued a *'Proposed Class Action Proceeding'* geared to clarify Constitutional Law that government would be more compliant in the best interest of all taxpayers.

It is plain Magna Carta principle for common good has not worked out too well in the long run. A huge divide between the superrich society and acutely poor is due to consequential math for those on receiving ends of revenue distributions from the budget balance billed in the middle— paid by a non-receiving middleclass.

The contrivance for a *'balanced budget'* is basic math, which sets up a variable tax rate on different classes.

Indeed manipulating rates to tax is fundamental to the capitalistic system intended for a democratic ideal of a commonwealth in the Charter for the Bank of England behind financial revolution and tax reform in 1694.

The bank system began to go wrong in 1697 when a run on the Bank forced it to suspend payment. And then in 1720, the most famous, *'South Sea Bubble'*;

'...a financial crisis in Britain arising out of speculation mania generated by Parliament's approval of the South Sea Company proposal to take over National Debt in exchange of its own stock for government bonds.' [2]

The financial revolution billed debt is money carried by future generations taxed as needed to bank tax funded money into circulation through countrywide banking. The system depended on the budget process to collect income tax behind government spending as voted by Members of Parliament to redistribute the wealth for common good from the commonwealth of the nation.

William Krehm was critical of Canadian government in his book, *'The Bank of Canada, A Power Unto Itself'*, published in 1993. It detailed his measure of concern about monetary policy to borrow from foreign banks rather than Bank of Canada loans for more economical money, and that tax redistributions were much more beneficial to the rich than taxpayers in their debt was disadvantage worth a lawsuit to resolve injustice.

Krehm described how money taxed in public account is re-taxed in private account, when a counterfeit tax-credit revalorizes public debt in private profits due to *'Double Presentment'* the way that lawyers sue it today.

~~~~~~~~~~~

---

[2] Ref: Cambridge Encyclopedia 2nd Edition: South Seas Bubble Page 812.

6. Committee on Monetary and Economic Reform

In May 2008, the Toronto Star reported William Krehm founder of the Committee on Monetary and Economic Reform (COMER) suing the Bank of Canada and the government in probably the best known constitutional challenge of law in Canadian legal history.

The newspaper quoted lawyer Rocco Galati for Krehm;

'It's going to be a significant challenge of the way the government has been using the Bank of Canada contrary to its enabling legislation. It will probably end up before the Supreme Court.'

Litigation was styled in the name of COMER being the publishing arm of a *'Think Tank'* created in the 1980s. Ann Emmett formed a COMER Steering Committee called Comer – Committee for Monetary and Economic Reform that 13 co-plaintiffs each claimed a nominal $10,000 each in the lawsuit, figured as personal harm on the private side of public monies lost.

The lawsuit took a while to prepare a case in review of taxation that if the government of Canada had used its Public Bank of Canada from 1974 to 2012; it would not have amassed C$500billion national debt, it would have saved some C$1trillion interest instead of cost of money paid to foreign banks, and there would have been an estimated C$13billion surplus in the budget.

The largest expenditure in the Federal Budget in 2012 was reported as interest paid private banks; more than national defense, or social security, or health care. The government invoked cuts and austerity measures that slashed programs by C$6b, purged 20,000 public jobs, and increased the retirement age of 65 to 67 to collect more from more people living longer working lives.

The Comer lawsuit was announced in a press release;

RESTORE THE USE OF THE BANK OF CANADA FOR THE BENEFIT OF CANADIANS AND REMOVE IT FROM THE CONTROL OF INTERNATIONAL PRIVATE ENTITIES WHOSE INTERESTS AND DIRECTIVES ARE PLACED ABOVE THE INTEREST OF CANADIANS AND THE PRIMACY OF THE CONSTITUTION OF CANADA

Canadian constitutional lawyer, Rocco Galati, on behalf of Canadians William Krehm, Ann Emmett, and COMER (Committee for Monetary and Economic Reform) on December 12th, 2011 filed an action in Federal Court, to restore the use of the Bank of Canada to its original purpose, by exercising its public statutory duty and responsibility. That purpose includes making interest free loans to municipal / provincial / federal governments for "human capital" expenditures (education, health, other social services) and /or infrastructure expenditures.

The action also constitutionally challenges the government's fallacious accounting methods in its tabling of the budget by not calculating nor revealing the true and total revenues of the nation before transferring back "tax credits" to corporations and other taxpayers.

The Plaintiffs state that since 1974 there has been a gradual but sure slide into the reality that the Bank of Canada and Canada's monetary and financial policy are dictated by private foreign banks and financial interests contrary to the Bank of Canada Act.

The Plaintiffs state that the Bank of International Settlements (BIS), the Financial Stability Forum (FSF) and the International Monetary Fund (IMF) were all created with the cognizant intent of keeping poorer nations in their place which has now expanded to all nations in that these financial institutions largely succeed in overriding governments and constitutional orders in countries such as Canada over which they exert financial control.

The Plaintiffs state that the meetings of the BIS and Financial Stability Board (FSB) (successor of FSF), their minutes, their discussions and deliberations are secret and not available nor accountable to Parliament, the executive, nor the Canadian public notwithstanding that the Bank of Canada policies directly emanate from these meetings. These organizations are essentially private, foreign entities controlling Canada's banking system and socio-economic policies.

The Plaintiffs state that the defendants (officials) are unwittingly and /or wittingly, in varying degrees, knowledge and intent engaged in a conspiracy, along with the BIS, FSB, IMF to render impotent the Bank of Canada Act as well as Canadian sovereignty over financial, monetary, and socioeconomic policy, and bypass the sovereign rule of Canada through its Parliament by means of banking and financial systems.

William Krehm was born of Canadian immigrant Jews from Russia in Toronto in 1913. He became an author, journalist, and one of the largest landlords in Toronto real estate in the O'Shanter Development Company. He was a political activist and he campaigned against government rent controls in the 1980s.

Krehm had been a Trotskyist in the 1930s and joined the US CLA – Communist League of America. He left the CLA and formed the Organizing Committee for a Revolutionary Workers Party allied with the IBRSP – International Bureau of Revolutionary Socialist Party. He fought in the Spanish Civil War with the POUM – Partido Obrero de Unificatión Marxista where he met author Eric Arthur Blair, best known, George Orwell.

Krehm was jailed in Spain as a spy, but was released after a hunger strike and returned to Canada in 1937. He toured the provinces talking about his experience in Spain. Time Magazine hired him as correspondent and he moved to Latin America in 1940.

The job lasted until 1947 when he was let go for being too critical of American politics in the region. He went back to Canada in 1948 and worked as a journalist, and then as a real estate developer, in the 1950s.

Krehm retired from O'Shanter and co-founded COMER – Committee on Monetary and Economic Reform in the 1980s. He published books on economics including; *'Babel's Tower'* in 1977 and *'A Power Unto Itself'* about the politics of the Bank of Canada in 1993.

Rent control was a political issue in the 1980s when Cadillac Fairview sold 11,000 apartment units to a Toronto trust company involving Rosenberg, Markle, and Player. The deal raised concern of rent increases due to *'pass-through'* mortgage costs to residents.

The Minister of Consumer and Commercial Relations announced an immediate audit with a Bill to limit the extent to which resale-mortgage costs could be passed on to rent-paying tenants. The Act was passed quickly as the province took possession of 3 trust companies; Greymac, Crown, and Seaway Trust. It held tenement units in receivership while investigations continued until each trust company was dissolved.

Aside from the COMER lawsuit worded from Krehm volumes, Comer developed education through monthly meetings for members, and planned public awareness sessions at venues in Canada, mostly in Toronto.

Ann Emmett, who knew of my experience in justice, asked me to assist Comer committee objectives with a report of the Bank of Canada system. I was asked to testify as an expert witness for COMER about Bank of Canada financials passed through the budget process.

I met Galati to confirm the undertaking for Comer and what he expected from me. He advised me to complete a JAD analysis and that he would inform me if and when bank system design would be required in court.

The media followed the COMER affair for several years. COMER had a Webpage, COMER was in newspapers, COMER was on Canadian radio and television news, and COMER was on talk shows in Canada and the USA where Paul Hellyer promoted his latest volume, *'Money Mafia'* with mention of the COMER lawsuit.

Hellyer was a former Acting Prime Minister of Canada in 1969 in a Liberal era. He became a popular speaker on US talk show Coasttocoastm as he talked about political intrigue and his version of conspiracy cloaked in ufology that aliens ruled the economy of the world.

~~~~~~~~~~~

7. Ruly English Words of Law to Command

My analysis of banking focused on money rules of law. I learnt legalese from lawyers in litigation and judges who rule the law how bankers create money and make it safe to expense through accepted Ways and Means.

The rule of law, which is coded for compliance, can be written in binary code that data processing computes inputs and outputs according to a sequential program in system language also written in words to command.

IT – Information Technology applies business rules to manage data and recordkeeping that system code controls computer processes which validate data inputs and outputs in operation. It is usually programmed to automate workflow, and dataflow, and cash flow.

Language evolved in the history of economic society to control people to do things for a price according to business and social norms written up in codes of law to command happenstance prescribed in Ruly English.

Ruly English is language that each word has a single meaning and each meaning a single word. Syntax is checked against ambiguity-avoiding rules that validate words for proper grammar and sequence in order that a sentence is clearly written to command what next.

Rules have roots in Royal Command of military orders and maneuvers and is used to control human behavior in many levels of society that social values are written in Code of Law how people live to work today.

Charters are written to stipulate professional conduct including; engineers, architects, lawyers, doctors, and various ways and means tested by accountants in the oversight of government agencies in charge of money.

Ruly English Words of Law Command Coded Ways and Means of a lawmaker Triune System Rules of Law that Regulation by Rules, and Enforcement of Rules, control Workflow, Dataflow, and Cash flow of serially connected Triune System Inputs and Outputs;

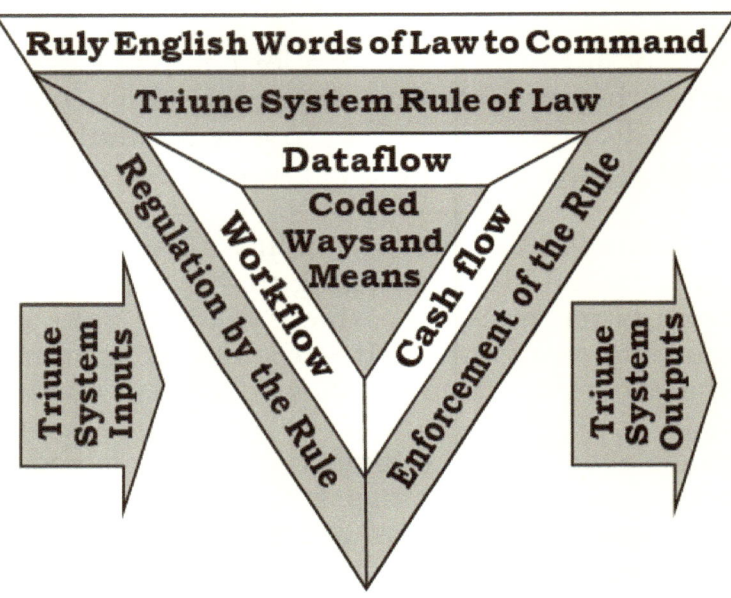

Triune— tripart law separates regulation from enforcement that compliance is largely a matter of power to rule to the extent authorities have jurisdiction. It may not be much as even proven secret commission loans tied to tax shelter sales geared to defraud tax revenue by design— the FCAC – Financial Consumer Agency of Canada has no power to intervene, it explained, the;

'Financial Consumer Agency of Canada does not have jurisdiction over contractual matters, or general service standards of the financial institutions it regulates. Legislation requires all federally regulated financial institutions to have in place a complaint handling process. Consumer concerns are important to us and we recommend you direct your complaint to the bank.'

Ruly English Words of Law to Command are legislated through government committees that issue codes of law to guide business management and judicial oversight. These are separate processes in place and time that span several procedure and reporting junctures.

Separation of law is called a spell, which may stretch a lifetime of legal wrangling before resolved, sometimes never. Instant *'Caught in the Act'* regulation includes photo-radar speed infractions measured and ticketed and fined and billed in computer automated processes that rule and enforce and penalize... in real time.

A key advantage of computerized ways and means is auditability that any disconnection, or disruption, or distortion compared to conformity, or responsibility, or accountability is retraceable through business metrics.

Legislation is rarely instantaneous that time is allowed for businesses to comply with orders as they happen in ways of change that to and fro in Bills of Law.

Still, time is crucial that the weakness of triune system rule of law is *'justice delayed is justice denied'*. And lenient judgments enfeeble to such extent that rulings fail to deter ongoing breaches of law. But not system binary code that unless actually arranged to defraud, computers have no interest in electronic pass-or-fail conditions that program to what is next.

Similarities between manual and automatic rules lie in how they are defined. Lawyers and programmers have special vocabulary to check triune system inputs and outputs to stipulate preprogrammed movements.

Monetary policy in the Bills of Exchange Act, 1882 was retrofitted to the Bank of England Act, 1694, which is more than 300 years old.

But the rapidity of the rate of change has increased exponential in the last 30 years. And, deregulation has the bad-bank side effect that downgrades compliance with ancient law how judges continue to rule from old NOTES OF LAW on this book cover from the past.

But that is history from the 1700s that Ruly English codified money rules of law in the 1800s. It was an enormous effort in the Bills of Exchange Act, 1882 that 100 laws were defined to protect the economy for the common good in the history of economic society.

But bankers have a different view of Ways and Means that notwithstanding the Bills of Exchange Act, 1882, all that matters is *'the bank is always right'* rule.

~~~~~~~~~~~

8. The Bank is Always Right Rule

The committee for COMER, Comer, organized events to discuss the lawsuit and teach economics from time to time. The organizers had pamphlets and books to sell from different authors, but mostly William Krehm.

Lessons focused on Canadian banking how Canada has a special place in economic history that Canadian money issued from Bank of Canada as a public bank is different than other G20 nations in Western Society, since its creation in 1937.

The cost of money in Canada around 1935 was about 30% of tax expenditures that William Lyon Mackenzie King lobbied to reduce in his campaign for election to be Prime Minister if people voted for the benefits of a Public Bank, which he broadcast on the radio,

"Once a nation parts with control of its currency and credit, it matters not who makes that nation's law. Usury, once in control, will wreck any nation. Until the control of the issue of currency and credit is restored to the government and recognized as its most conspicuous and sacred responsibility, all talk of sovereignty of Parliament and of democracy is idle and futile."

The Bank of Canada was founded as a Public Bank in the Constitution in 1938. Its mandate to lend to the government at near zero cost of money in the public interest of Canadians continued until around 1974. It issued cheap money with usury returned to the public purse. Canada prospered on this formula with a better economic experience than other nations in the G20.

Canada thrived on public interest in government to;

'Promote economic and financial welfare of Canada'.

The system funded federal projects that Minister of Finance, Charles Avery Dunning made payments to provinces with interest to the Bank of Canada repaid to people through the Treasury.

The Canadian economy outperformed other countries and Members of Parliament asked several rhetorical questions in the House of Commons that restated the obvious financial benefit quoted from Hansard Record,

"Will you tell me why the government with power to create money should give that power away to a private monopoly and then borrow that which Parliament can create itself, back at interest?"

First Governor of the Bank of Canada, Graham Towers defined banking how credits offset to debits made new money from counting assets in the credit column,

"The manufacturing process consists of making a pen-and-ink, or typewriter, entry on a card in a book."

He said from experience, adding a note of caution,

"...Now, if Parliament wants to change the form of operating the bank system, then certainly that is within the power of Parliament."

Whatever dangers the Prime Minister and Governor of the Bank of Canada might have worried about in the mid-1940s, bankers came down against it in the 60s.

They lobbied to amend the Bills of Exchange Act, 1882.

Section 165(3) entitled, *'An Act to amend the Bills of Exchange Act, 14-15 Eliz. II, S.C. 1966, c. 12, s. 4.'* had the bad-bank effect that suing on a cheque credited to its customer's account— *'the bank is always right'*;

Minister of Finance, Mitchell Sharp introduced the Bill to amend section 165(3) tabled by M. Jean Chrétien, M.P., to Bill S-14 [3] in the House of Commons Standing Committee of Finance, Trade and Economic Affairs, on March 24th, 1966, [4]

> *'Where a cheque is delivered to a bank for deposit to the credit of a person and the bank credits him with the amount of the cheque, the bank acquires all the rights and powers of a holder in due course of the cheque.'*

Banks also railed against government policy to use Public Bank of Canada low cost of money as it forced private banks to lend at a similar low rate of interest to compete. This changed when Pierre Elliott Trudeau, Prime Minister, agreed to comply with the demands of the BIS – Bank of International Settlements in 1974.

Parliament did not change the Bank of Canada remit, but simply chose to borrow its money from overseas.

The BIS is exclusively organized that no director shall be a government official, or a member of a legislative body, unless also being a governor of a central bank.

When Parliament ceded to the BIS, the government borrowed from private creditors at the higher offshore interest cost to print onshore money, instead of a low interest rate cost of money from its own Public Bank.

The policy lifted public debt to a second highest level of any previous Canadian Prime Minister. It increased a sustainable C$13<u>billion</u> <u>surplus</u> to an unsustainable C$650<u>billion</u> <u>deficit</u> through the millennium, when the cost of money at 20% was 91% of the budget in 1993.

---

[3] An act to amend the Bills of Exchange Act, 1st Sess., 27th Par., 1966
[4] http://lawjournal.mcgill.ca/userfiles/other/1642783-scott.pdf

It wasn't just the high cost of money, the 1980s and 90s were heydays for racketeers that the 20% cost of borrowed principal debt doubled in just 4 years. The Canadian Auditor General stated the problem in 1993,

"...most of the government debt consisted of interest charges."

COMER pleadings for trial were heard in 2012. The court was well attended with Comer members and so many others they had to find a bigger courtroom.

The court denied trial that COMER appealed in 2013.

New pleadings were filed and heard in 2014, which produced a new court order to amend the claim for yet another hearing for trial, scheduled out to 2015.

I learnt about the Public Bank of Canada from more than just reading COMER volumes. Comer asked me to write a book review of *'The Public Bank Solution'* by Ellen Brown which is highly regarded research. My review was published in many places including the UK British Green Party Webpage across the Atlantic.

As I studied the Bank of Canada for Comer I replied to calls for papers to attend conferences. And, I joined INET – Institute for New Economic Thinking at the Toronto *'Human After All'* Conference in 2014.

Former Prime Minister, Paul Martin was on the INET agenda, and we talked about the Finance Committee Report, which I took from my briefcase to remind him of my part in his budget. Professor Larry Summers, former US Treasury Secretary, was about to speak and we met in the conference hallway. He remembered me from our work in the WSJ Future of Finance Initiative, which we discussed at the White House in 2009.

Prof Summers gave an interesting after dinner speech, and then took questions from the audience.

I expressed my appreciation of the conference in my question, and I asked the professor to explain the problem of *'Rent Seeking Tax Arbitrage'* how it involved criminal banking, which he said as follows,

"The American journalist Mike Kinsley put forth the doctrine that the real scandal isn't usually the illegal things people do, it's the things that are fully legal. And that is certainly true with respect to tax sheltering and overseas tax sheltering and tax sheltering by financial institutions. Tax shelters tax arbitrage comes in forms that are mind numbingly complex. But, its essence is that you borrow money and you deduct the interest on your borrowing and you put the money somewhere where you earn interest and you don't pay tax on the interest you earn. And, if you do those two things at the same rate and you can subtract you recognize you make a profit that's equal to the tax rate times the interest rate on each dollar of your money. And, there's no question that there's a lot of that that goes on. There's no question that but for successful rent-seeking in individual countries there would be substantially less of it. There's no question that to fully address it would require more international cooperation than we have now. And, there's no question that it is a very serious problem, as I tried to convey when I spoke about the dark side of capital mobility. I have no doubt there are tens if not hundreds of billions of dollars that should be collected by the world's fiscs that are not, because of the kinds of tax arbitrage activities that you describe."

It seemed to me, the *'dark side of capital mobility'* from a former US Treasury Secretary described the COMER claim. It was just as big a problem in Canada as it was in the USA, indeed, the world over.

William Krehm and Ann Emmett, both senior citizens for COMER and Comer filed a Canadian Class Action for all taxpayers to have their day in court.

Comer hosted a *'Money, Tax, and Poverty'* Conference on January 24, 2015 at the Toronto City Hall. It was the Saturday just ahead of COMER pleadings for trial on Monday, January 26, 2015.

Councilor Christine Wong Tam launched the session with opening remarks about money and the benefits of using the Bank of Canada as its own Public Bank.

I introduced Ann Emmett who followed with a keynote address on behalf of Comer. Then speakers including; Mike Palecek, Canada Postal Workers Union described Post Office Banks, Al Rosen, author of *'Swindlers'* and *'Easy Prey Investors'* about securities fraud. I spoke of myself as witness for COMER in my presentation of Ponzi banking in a technical presentation. After that, I introduced Rocco Galati as our special guest as people wanted to hear all about the COMER lawsuit.

Galati for COMER referred to history as he described the case with respect to money and bank fraud,

"It's a Constitutional challenge to the Bank of Canada and the Minister of Finance in refusing to give interest free loans to the Federal and Provincial governments, which was the central reason the bank was set up in 1937."

Galait spoke about tax the same as Larry Summers,

"The other part of the challenge, which goes hand-in-hand with this whole banking fraud that's going on, is against the Minister of Finance and the budgetary process."

Galati explained the budget process tax accounting in terms of Magna Carta principle,

"Since 1215, and the Magna Carta, because only parliament can impose taxes, parliament will not impose taxes, cannot impose taxes before the government tells the House of Commons how it plans to spend that money in the next session. The speech from the throne is a constitutional requirement before the budget is actually passed. The problem with the budget in our country is a sleight of hand goes on."

Galati talked through distorted Ways and Means,

"To give you an example, they'll say our expenditure needs are 280 billion, we're going to have revenue of 240 billion, therefore we need to borrow 40 billion and that's our deficit for the year."

Then Galati explained the crafty political makings of Magna Carta Loophole Gullible Taxpayer Law,

"Well that's not true, they collect, or could collect a lot more than that, but then they transfer back to taxpayers, running from everyone from the single mother, or single parent, to mega corporations."

He paused, to emphasize the point,

"They transfer back... money... in tax credits, and then they say we have 240 billion, we need to spend 280."

Galati disparaged Parliament, and belittled politicians, as simple minded people lacking intelligence required to figure out how to balance the tax budget,

"The MPs should know that, because then they can have an intelligent..."

"...if they're capable, I don't know, maybe half of them couldn't do it... but, if they could have an intelligence debate, on whether, or not, they want to run a $40billion deficit, or shave the tax credits, and run a balanced budget."

And, then because Galati represented COMER in the lawsuit to close a tax loophole, ending,

"And so, that's a very nasty sleight of hand that's going on with our budgetary process, which I... we say is unconstitutional."

So, there it was... Galati explained the Bank of Canada conspiracy theory on public record with only 36 hours before a second pleading for trial in court on Monday.

The Conference that was attended by more than 300 people ended in public interest of a panel discussion.

I printed drafts of Crawford's Pocket Money to Ruly English Dictionary to take to the Federal Court of Canada where I met Paul Hellyer, William Krehm, and Ann Emmett after the hearing to give them an early edition in a photo-op for the record.

Galati was as passionate about COMER as Emmett was about Comer. They educated the public about the lawsuit and banking and the budget and they were both acknowledged for their good work. The Canadian Alliance of Seniors recognized Ann Emmett with an Alex Gorlick Humanitarian Award in May 2017. And the Ontario Bar Association presented Galati with the President's Award, about the same time.

~~~~~~~~~~~

9. Wisdom of Lawmakers is no Concern of the Law

Galati amended the COMER lawsuit to sue declaratory relief that would clarify ancient law for politicians, and Canadians like me less trusting of our bankers.

The COMER case before the Federal Court of Canada alleged government breach of constitutional law.

Lawyer, Rocco Galati for William Krehm and COMER sued to restore the use of the public Bank of Canada to its original purpose to issue cheap money in the best public interest of Canadian taxpayers, versus the private interest of foreign banks behind a criminally rigged LIBOR – London Inter-Bank Offered Rate.

The Public Bank of Canada was a uniquely Canadian opportunity lost when the Liberal Party chose to issue money on loan through the BIS. But, the Conservative Party also endorsed it, promoting a *'New World Order'* as if Canada could not be left out of global affairs.

COMER alleged Parliament acted above law, which the CBC - Canadian Broadcasting Corporation questioned on *'The Exchange'* when the host-interviewer asked Galati, what he hoped for from the ruling? He said,

"My hope is that the Court declare that the government is bound by the legislation. It cannot simply handover that decision making to foreign private bankers."

The COMER Action also alleged fallacious accounting of tax credits hidden from the Treasury not reported in the budget. Galati was very clear in his pleadings for trial, that the real case before the court was fake accounting that distorted the budget in Parliament in breach of *'no taxation without representation'* Magna Carta principle.

Galati was not involved in Comer monthly meetings, but he attended COMER General Meetings to report progress of litigation as the lawyering continued.

One day, Galati tested lawsuit claimants at a COMER meeting with a riddle, which in old Roman law was a way to test the analytical skills of a lawyer in court;

'Three people bought 3 $10 meals for $25 in a deal that each paid a ten dollar bill. The cashier put $30 in the till giving $5 in change of five loonies which the waiter put on the table. Each diner picked up a loonie that 3 x $10 - $1 is 3 times $9 is $27, which from $30 leaves $3, but there was only two loonies on the table, which is $2.'

Galati pondered, *"Where did the missing dollar go?"*

The lawyer asked each claimant in turn, but none of them could say who took the dollar. He explained it as fallacious accounting. But it demonstrated the gap between COMER litigants suing for legal clarification, and committee claimants suing $10,000 on account of losses none of them could really explain if asked.

The justice system was as slow as reputed to be that 4 years passed until Galati presented the amended claim for COMER for trial in court October 14, 2015.

Justice Russell heard from Peter Hajecek, lawyer for the Crown who referred to the budget and taxation,

"I will quickly move to budget presentation and taxation, which is paragraph 12 and it is page 189 of the record."

Justice Russell found the material,

"Right. I'm there."

Hajecek established the foundation of his arguments,

"Here, My Lord, I will seek to make three points: first, that there is no constitutional duty in presenting the budget in the manner that the Plaintiffs urge upon the Court; that in any event, what was— what has been done in Canada for some time and what was done, I guess, if I can call it the material time, there was no breach of the principle of no taxation without representation; and thirdly, that Parliament is master of its own process."

Hajecek expanded the first point,

"...there's no constitutional duty of presenting the federal budget to Parliament in a manner sought by the Plaintiffs, and the truth of the matter, My Lord, is that the Plaintiffs are not able to point to a constitutional provision, a section of the Constitution or a section of the Charter that says this is the way the Minister of Finance must present the budget."

Hajecek picked up on his second point,

"...there is no breach of the principle of no taxation without representation. This starts at paragraph 12 of the factum. The principle of no taxation without representation is codified in section 53 of the Constitution Act. That principle, I submit, means that there may not be any taxation federally unless the tax is levied with the authority of Parliament. And respectfully, there is no pleading that it wasn't done in this case. So there has been no breach with respect to the budget."

The Crown concluded to explain power of Parliament,

"The third point I wish to make is that Parliament is master of its own procedure."

The lawyer for the Crown referred to doctrine and the spirit of the Magna Carta in the law,

"First after all, in this country, the doctrine of legitimate expectations, the best that can do is it will grant procedure rights. ...My friend makes reference to the Magna Carta, which we know just celebrated— of course there were many Magna Carta(s), but the one from 1215 just celebrated its 800th anniversary."

"...Our position is that it is important in a legal landscape, but it doesn't really bind, and it can be, it's amenable to ordinary legislative change. Our submission is that it doesn't assist the Plaintiffs to say, well, there is something like this in the Magna Carta."

The judge questioned Ways and Means of Parliament,

"So if a bill comes before Parliament and the information is defective, I mean there is not enough information in it to make a meaningful decision, the remedy is what? You're telling me this..."

Hajecek answered with respect to democratic process,

"Well, I guess the remedy is this, is that we have elections every at least five years, the Constitution mandates. So the remedy would be is that people would vote in a party that would pass a different law."

Court observers laughed at the absurdity a vote would resolve unconstitutionality, as the lawyer continued,

"Now this, of course, subject that there are no constitutional problems with the law, which we are quite aware, that the law doesn't appear to ask state actors to enact in a way which would be subject to judicial review."

Justice Russell used the moment for clarification,

"So, are you saying if Parliament wishes to pass legislation without having the full wherewithal, the full knowledge of what the legislation is all about, that's okay?"

Hajecek described the political power of lawmakers to frame his submission with respect to the budget,

"That is up to Parliament, because, my next point is that Parliament is supreme in its deliberations."

The lawyer for the Crown quoted the law,

"Parliamentary privilege consists of the rights and immunities which the two houses of Parliament and their members and officers possess to enable them to carry out their parliamentary functions effectively. Without this protection, members would be handicapped in performing their parliamentary duties, and the authority of Parliament itself in confronting the executive and as a forum for expressing the anxieties of citizens would be correspondingly diminished."

The judge had asked the lawyer for the Crown for an account of the law, which was an education to me,

"So, my submission to you is what could be more important to Parliament's functioning than the debate of the budget? The processing of the budget, and that's why in our Constitution it's very clear in the Constitution Act, 1867, that it must be in the House of Commons."

Justice Russell wanted more clarification,

"So in, in blunt terms, you're telling me if Parliament wished to act in an incompetent way, that's, that's up to Parliament?"

Hajecek was cautious as to what to say,

"Well, your Lordship is certainly using blunt words. It's not for me to say whether, these are..."

Justice Russell made allowances for candor,

"No I'm, I'm pitching it at a hypothetical."

Hajecek appreciated the segue,

"Yes. Yes, exactly. That's right. I would prefer that. As an officer of the Crown I would prefer that, is, er..."

The Defense for the Crown spoke to an example from history books of law that the public rarely reads,

Let's put it this way: It's like, it's like this idea of parliamentary intent which we all search for when we do Charter analyses, and there's a great British jurist who said, "You know that's really a 'Will o' Wisp'. They all have various intents, those individual members who were representing their ridings, and they may have different intents at various steps," er..."

"Er, at various, you know, first reading when it comes back from committee, so I guess what I am trying to say is that it may not have seemed so to those members, but the way our Constitution works is they make the laws. Once the laws are on the books it... our judiciary scrutinizes them for conformity with the Constitution..."

The lawyer for the Crown chose his words carefully to speak to the democratic purpose of judiciary,

"But... But, um, wisdom is not something that, wisdom of legislation is not in the bailiwick of courts, as I understand it."

Hajecek referred to what the Court says,

"How the legislative body proceeds is a matter that is immune from judicial review and a matter of self-definition and inherent authority of the legislative body. That is in my factum and so is the quote. There are various views that this originates with article 9 of the Bill of Rights of 1688-89."

Hajecek questioned the incorporated association,

"So the first point is that section 3 of the Charter rights can only be held by citizens, and one of the Plainfiff here is a corporation. So an incorporated association. Section 3 says every citizen of Canada has the right to vote in an election of members of the House of Commons or a legislative assembly, and to be qualified for membership therein."

Hajecek defined representation and participation,

"Now, clearly, on the face of it that's a very narrow right. It's a grant to each citizen to vote and to run for office. So our courts do Charter analysis. They look at the purpose of the right. But my submission to Your Lordship this morning is that our courts have identified the content of section 3 a conferring on each Canadian citizen the right to effective representation and to meaningful participation."

"And further, my submission is that it has never been interpreted by our courts to encompass any kind of a right or expectation that there will be a particular electoral outcome, or that the representatives who have been elected would enact or fail — or refrain from enacting any particular measure or tax."

Hajecek quoted law about representation in Canada,

"Ours is a representative democracy. Each citizen", which is underlined, *"is entitled to be represented in government. Representation comprehends the idea of having a voice in the deliberations of government as well as the idea of the right to bring one's grievances and concerns to the attention of one's government representative."*

Hajecek put the ruling in context for the Court,

"Representative, singular. So we say that is one component of the right to vote, the right to represented. And we say that was not breached here. An understanding of section 3 emphasizes the right of each citizen to play a meaningful role in the electoral process is also... of a full range of reasons that individuals participate in the electoral process, and that is why it is of such importance to a free and democratic society."

Justice Russell agreed,

"That's true. But I, er, once again I... the bottom, your bottom line I think is you're telling me if you have a problem with what occurred here, here, your complaint should be to your representative and not to the court."

"That's exactly it, yeah... Yeah, that's my submission."

Hajacek had more to say about declaratory relief,

"The claim for declaratory relief, this was found in the Crown factum beginning at paragraph 42. And I think what's important is language that we use and yes, in a theoretical sense, a person can seek declaratory relief as to the meaning of legislation which certainly sounds like, absent a factual matrix they are asking for an advisory opinion. So in a theoretical sense they can, but they must satisfy a test."

He explained how the relief-test is discretionary,

"Yes, theoretically it's possible, because I don't know whether it's theoretically possible here and whether it's actually possible in the Federal Court. But there is a question about that, and I know that the test for me is plain and obvious…"

Hajecek admitted to the law being so convoluted that to clarify would be difficult test,

"And it's pretty hard with any kind of jurisdiction question in the Court, I would submit— no disrespect intended— but given our laws to make it plain and obvious?"

Hajecek questioned real verses theoretical interest quoting from the previous ruling,

"I see no private rights at issue. In addition they claim to be acting for", quote, "all other Canadians. But once again they have yet to produce pleadings that adequately plead how the rights of", quote, "all other Canadians", and all is underscored, "have been impacted in a way that translates into the infringement of an individual or collective right. If the rights of all", which is underscored, "Canadians are impacted, then the individual Plaintiffs will be able to describe in accordance with the rules of government pleadings how their individual rights have been breached, but they have as yet not been able to do this."

"So that was the Court's view in April 2014. And it's my submission that that governs. So the question before you today is how the Plaintiffs through amendment has been able to describe what Your Lordship found to be wanting in the claim as it was before the Court in April 2014."

Hajecek quoted the exclusory nature of treaties,

"This makes sense, as the factors underlying the decision to sign a treaty are beyond the courts' ken or capability to assess, and any assessment of them would take courts beyond their proper role within the separation of powers."

Hajecek described COMER with respect to a treaty,

"So why am I making this point? COMER doesn't plead, it's clear that COMER has an issue with the Canadian participation in certain foreign banks and institutions. It's not clear to me in the pleadings what is being taken issue with. Is the issue being taken with executive decision to enter into a treaty, to be a member of those institutions? Because if that's it, then we would say by virtue of what I have just read to the Court that could not go forward as not justiciable."

Hajecek argued that delegation is not abdication,

"As we know, during the First World War and during the Second World War Parliament delegated extensive powers to the Governor-in-Council while this country was at war. If you read that, it says, yeah, it can pretty well delegate all its powers except the power to take it back. ...it stands for the principle that the delegation by Parliament of its powers — to the Governor-in Council is pretty wide."

Justice Russell questioned about specific delegation,

"From your perspective, what do you see has been delegated here?"

Hajecek hedged in political sense that he did not know what had been delegated,

"I'm not sure, you see, because that is my friend's pleading. They say there has been this improper handing off. I don't know what has been handed off. There is talk about that things were done no longer in the best interest of Canadians. Now, I always thought that Canadians get to decide at least every five years what is in their best interest."

The lawyer for the Crown recommending remedial use of the vote had people laughing, as he soldiered on,

"That is why we have elections. Gosh, we sure hope so. So I am not sure what the delegation is. The point I am seeking to meet is this: Is whatever my friend says it is, or whatever the Plaintiffs say it is, the law, the law which he has cited states that the delegation can be so wide that I'm having a problem with the issue that something is delegated."

"If the Supreme Court in Grey has said, Parliament, you can delegate if you deem it necessary to the Governor-in-Council pretty well everything, pretty well all powers except the power to take all those powers back. That is the point I am trying to make. Not knowing what supposedly is being delegated, I'm just saying..."

Justice Russell paraphrased the problem,

"Yes, all right. So what you're saying it's so broad, whatever happened here, it's..."

"Yeah whatever supposedly happened, is — yeah, would not be infringing this. Because my friend is finding this, right? He is finding this interstitially. He's not pointing to a section of the Constitution Act. He it's pointing to a section of the Charter, but my submission to you is that section 3 only goes as far as it has been interpreted in this country."

And then finally, Hajecek argued that COMER had no private standing as an incorporated company,

"...it is a teaching which takes a three-part test for public interest standing, and I don't think... and I think the Court agreed with me before that there isn't a private standing here. The public interest standing, it's a three-part test. Part of that test is justiciability. But the main part of the test is... or I would say to focus on is: Is this the best way? Is this the best way to bring this issue to the Court?"

Hajecek advised how to challenge the Bank of Canada,

"But here we would submit to you that there are much better ways to bring this. An institution that is denied a loan, if in fact there is a duty to make loans— that would be the perfect place to challenge— to seek to see what section 18 of the Bank of Canada really means, whether "may" actually means "should". So I fully admit the test is flexible and discretionary, and our submission is that there are better ways and also that these kinds of challenges should really be brought, I think in a factual matrix... That is the way that courts traditionally like to approach things, is to have a factual matrix, something they can get their teeth into, rather than sort of making a general statement about what a provision may mean."

Crown pleadings against trial of bank law continued to a break in proceedings when Galati had his turn to argue for COMER to have its day in court. But, the trouble with unreal money is that the rich know how to break the law to make real money, and on whom, and where to spend it, to profit with want to keep it.

~~~~~~~~~~~

10. Court Ordered Debt in Justice

If it had not been for William Krehm and Rocco Galati for COMER, and Ann Emmett Chair of Comer, I would not have analyzed banking to follow tax credits hidden from the Treasury not reported in the budget.

I would not have learnt Ruly English. I would not have defined bank system workflow, dataflow and cash flow, or Ways and Means to make money from a promise to repay made-up credit used in my name. And, I would not have written a dissertation for peer review.

As contrived as TIC Products were for tax avoidance, and as much as LIBOR was criminal that banks rigged the interest cost of money for illegal profits, the bank effect of making sense fake money was made to thieve.

In 2005, the IRS in the USA issued a public warning;

'Abusive trust arrangements will not produce the tax benefits advertised by their promoters.'

Debt followed the crash in such amounts in the news that Justice Echlin noted an *'epidemic'* of bad loans in litigation to collect in 2009. Still, the party line said Canada had been saved from financial ruin because of strongly regulated banking— compared to overseas.

Some governments announced taxpayers had to save bank debt. Portugal, Italy, and Greece a so-called PIG crisis zone positioned Greece the worst financial out-of-its depth country in the Global Credit Crunch.

Canada was quite stoic about notional national debt. Vancouver, Calgary, Edmonton, Saskatoon, Winnipeg, Toronto, Ottawa, Montreal, Fredericton, and Halifax, and other Canadian cities reported some $100b losses.

Hamilton, not far away, estimated $14m paper losses due to $97m holdings in ABCP.

My concern was *'Signature-Specific-Identity-Theft'* that Hamilton, MPP Andrea Horwath, read in Petition 44,

Hamilton Center... "Thank you Speaker, this Petition is for potential debtors identity validation and financial due diligence that will safeguard peoples' wealth and equity in property from fraudulent loan applications, specifically in cases of third party representation using notarized affidavits by, or for, loan handling lawyers that may benefit themselves and, or, their affiants."

NDP Leader, Jack Layton had signed Petition 44 to re-open an OSC file to investigate securities fraud, but there was no news of it, and still nothing happened.

All I wanted was public debate for transparent banking a transaction control number would solve the problem.

That was my analysis in letters to Prime Ministers that lack of oversight allowed ABCP Sponsors and ABCP Distribution Agents and ABCP Sales Reps to collude in tax deductible securities fraud. I didn't know it was a legal amendment to the Bills of Exchange Act, 1882.

Bay Street, Purdy Crawford was assigned to the Pan-Canadian Investors Committee to settle a debt crisis.
The first part of the plan was to stay lawsuits to settle ABCP debt around August 2007 after the huge paper sell-off triggered bank failures including Wall Street Lehman Brothers real estate mortgage derivatives.

ABCP *'Holders'* agreed to a Montreal Accord in August 2007 that instead of selling ABCP Third-Party Notes at a loss, banks could sue for judgment of law to collect.

The Pan-Canadian Investors Committee formulated a plan in December 2007. Purdy Crawford announced a Montreal Accord in the news for a meeting at the Royal York Hotel, which is where I met him in March 2008.

He described his plan to rescue institutional investors holding 99% of $32b ABCP in pension plans. He said 1% in retail was more difficult that some 1800 people, including me, had lost more than $400m.

The Chairman explained how the Committee had used the CCAA – Companies Creditors Arrangement Act and its Chapter 11 section to incorporate ABCP to add new value to a pool of assets with an equalization formula and marginal funding geared to reduce future losses. He said it was a CCAA first to recapitalize investments. The audience had questions about which banks were at risk and I recall he said BMO was the most exposed. He said ABCP had been sold without transparency, which made it difficult to pinpoint liabilities.

Chairman Crawford described ABCP to be a kind of *'Creative Destruction'* quoting Warren Buffet, *"You only know who's swimming naked when the tide goes out"*.

After his presentation I introduced myself that I had a question. It was still 2008 and lawyers had told me tax scams had nothing to do with the ABCP that Purdy Crawford was talking about. I told him I had signed an Investor Note which I had already paid in a failed tax shelter scheme at my loss. I asked him if he thought I had signed an ABCP promissory note, but he said he couldn't say. So, I asked about bank reform and need for transparency, which he said wasn't his mandate.

I gave him a copy of my *'Perfect Sting'* how we posed as two Crawford's together in a photograph, and I never saw him again.

The Committee reaches agreement in principle in June 2008 and the Ontario Superior Court approved a plan in August 2008 to restructure imaginary ABCP tax-credit value to reconvert to real money.

The Ontario Superior Court of Justice approved the Pan-Canadian plan to restructure ABCP in June 2008.

Retail investors objected to being excluded and they sued for a better deal in the Ontario Superior Court. But, this was also rejected by the Court in August 2008. They appealed to the Supreme Court of Canada, in September 2008, but that Court refused to hear it.

The Pan-Canadian Investors Committee created a new deal in December 2008 which was given final approval in the Ontario Superior Court in January 2009.

It was a deal that bankers were not prosecuted, and no one went to jail, although it was often questioned if the debt was created through *'Shadow Banking'*;

'Bank-like activities mainly lending, conducted through non-regulated entities, including hedge funds, money market funds, and securitization vehicles. The shadow banking system also refers to unregulated activities by regulated institutions. It has been common practice for investment banks to conduct many of their transaction in ways that don't show up on their conventional balance sheet accounting and so are not visible to regulators. To the extent that investment banks do this, they can be considered part of the shadow banking system.' [5]

~~~~~~~~~~~

---

[5] Ref: The Public Bank Solution. Third Millennium Press, June 2013 by Ellen Brown, Shadow Banking System Page 437.

11. Signature-Specific Identity Theft

Aside from the CRA and ICAO decisions against Perris found guilty of professional misconduct selling tax scams for 11 years before he was caught, he was also sued by the bank that paid him for his witnessing of people signing Windbills— one of which was his wife.

It seems Perris knew the law to deal with the bank. He challenged it to prove it paid a secret commission for his witness of his wife signing a tax-scam deal that depended on a secret bank loan to close and operate;

'The defendants further deny the amounts due and owing as claimed and puts the Plaintiff to the strict proof thereof. The Defendants therefore submit that this Action be dismissed with costs.'

Perris and his lawyer threatened to be whistleblowers of secret commission tied loan that the bank chose not to sue. But it sued others, like me, who had no idea what Perris had done, or how deregulated banking is geared to defraud, or how a Windbill works.

Perris and his lawyer knew what I didn't know— that *'one law for the rich and another for the poor'* is law in Canada in section 165(3). Perris put it in reverse as he could name-and-shame the bank if it sued to collect a loan to one of its own that conned securities fraud.

The bank sued me for a similar loan that Perris had put one in my name and another in my wife's name we knew nothing about until the bank sued its first to collect. My defense was to blame Perris, except I had to prove it involved *'Signature-Specific-Identity-Theft'*. My lawyer advised me to follow the money, which was easy when the bank filed system design in its defense of unnumbered comingled loans in a conduit account.

I included a legend of steps to follow workflow dataflow and cash flow by numbers through the bank system;

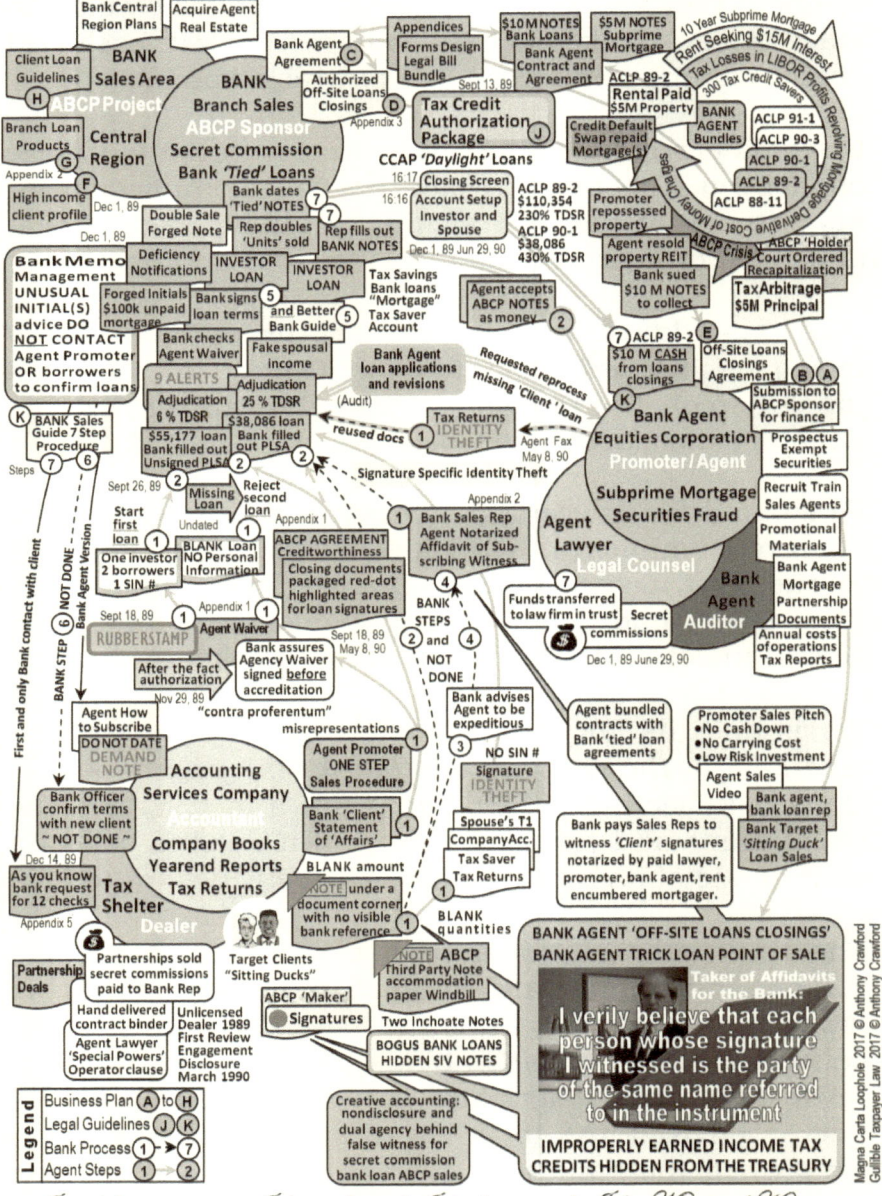

As a computer system engineer I knew how to decipher workflow in flowchart symbols to back-engineer the code that automated bank *'Off-Site Loans Closings'*. It showed a BWAB – Bank Within a Bank workflow from a front office in the bottom right where Sales Reps sign Affidavits of Subscribing Witness notarized by a Bank Agent *'Taker of Affidavits'* of an oath sworn to deceive;

'I verily believe that each person whose signature I witnessed is the party of the same name referred to in the instrument'.

It underpinned a *'Signature-Specific-Identity-Theft'*.

Prof John Chant had defined job titles in his study for the government 2009 ABCP *'Crisis in Canada'* Report, which I reapplied to my detailed workflow based on his ABCP *'Acquire-to-Distribute'* business model.

The workflow showed an ABCP Sponsor in the top left where a bank targeted a so-called *'Sitting Duck'* in the bottom left for a namesake loan given a tax-saver who signed blank promissory notes at the Point of Sale. The ABCP Distribution Agent notarized a sworn oath from sales reps who signed Affidavits of Subscribing Witness for the bank, which used them to set up tied loans to close each sale that paid a secret commission to anyone in the financial sector willing to defraud.

'Double Presentment Twice Paid Tax Credit Windbill Workflow' starts in bank procedure ① to ⑦ steps and bank agent ❶ to ❷ in procedure steps. The bank filled out a PLSA – Personal Loan Service Application for a secret commission loan through accreditation advised to the ABCP Sales Rep for the amount to fill out on the ABCP Sponsor bank loan demand note afforded to the ABCP Distribution Agent amount filled out as ABCP liability to a CDS – Credit Default Swap *'Investor Note'*.

Bank processes ended in steps ⑥ and ⑦ that the bank should have, but did not confirm client loans afforded to me to invest in tax shelter units. It continued on to date demand notes for secret commission tied loans, used to close sales through *'Off-site Loans Closings'*.

Perris was found guilty, without prosecution, receiving referral fees tied to loans to sell tax shelter schemes that couldn't be sold or defraud without them.

Lawyers gave me legalese to add to system analysis as they spelled their words from Black's dictionary of law; *'Contra Proferentum'* is an ambiguity doctrine, and I found *'Money'* and *'Windmill'* for *'Kiting'* imaginary credit how it raises real money from unreal *'Debt'* as it is defined in Thomson's dictionary of banking'.

My lawyer told me to find as much evidence as I could for a good defense. Data analysis might not have been expected and the more they asked, the more I charted. But, the more I told them what they seemed to already know, the more nervous they got to sue to defense.

The bank denied a secret circle of funds from tied loan dependent securities fraud to profit from cash flow in top right workflow analysis of codependent promissory notes. There was so much evidence of wrongdoing that a lawyer quit the case to defend, so a judge ruled debt without trial with summary judgment for the bank to collect. The ruling dismissed claims and counterclaims that the bank saved Perris from another prosecution.

Not many Financial Advisors were coddled like Perris.

But Perris, as a bank paid witness, was a small fish in big pond, and I began to think legalese is a language of lies that set me apart from sensible conversation with lawyers, which all but disappeared.

When the CRA sued a client of Perris drawn into his *'Art Flip'* caper, a judge ruled Perris in a fiduciary relationship with his client, and in breach of obligation by obtaining a secret commission in the deal. Perris was ordered to refund his $7.500 referral fee in 2004.

But judgment to repay a secret commission referral fee did not remove the private debt obligation, and the real victim of tax fraud is still the taxpayer who pays public debt to recapitalize an improperly earned tax credit.

If the CRA had sued me to repay a tax-credit Windbill note in his tax shelter real estate scheme, I would have figured out my private and public losses sooner.

Signature-specific identity theft is modern counterfeit;

*'**402.2 (1)** Identity Theft – Everyone commits an offence who knowingly obtains or possesses another person's identity information in the circumstances of giving rise to a reasonable inference that the information is intended to be used to commit an indictable offence that includes fraud, deceit or falsehood as an element of the offence.'*

Law defines crime that people have to be careful what they sign does not create a contingent debt, especially if those in positions of trust sign signatures for people for the sake of convenient banking. [6]

The wheels of justice turned slowly and the lawyering went on for about 12 years in my case, and about 6 years for COMER until neither me nor Krehm had our day in court. Trial was simply ruled out with hardly subjective reasons or no reason at all for COMER.

---

[6] CANADIAN PRESS Calgary (CP) the Investment Dealers Association has imposed a $100,000 fine and assessed $15,000 in costs against a BMO Nesbitt Burns investment advisor who allowed his assistant to forge his own, and client, signatures between November 1996 and June 2001, contrary to an IDA bylaw.

In my 12 year legal process I learnt amazing tricks that lawyers used to deny trial of my analysis of what the RCMP – Royal Canadian Mounted Police described as potentially criminal banking. It was referred to the Police that also refused to investigate.

My lawyer said there was no criminal code to charge Perris and the OSC still refused to investigate what they called a civil matter.

The bank examined me twice and a third time with all the lawyers acting for defendants in my counterclaim. I had to file a motion for a court order to examine the bank, but I was never allowed to question Perris.

If there was vindication it was around May 2008 when the court ruled against trial of the bank in my case, it might have been my evidence of tied-loan securities fraud led to an investigation of those involved.

An investment planning corporation was investigated that a deal was made when the company admitted to having failed to establish policies and procedures to ensure clients qualified as accredited investors (in accordance with provisions of the Ontario Securities Act) before purchases of prospect exempt securities. It paid a $65,000 fine and $10,000 costs in May 2010.

It didn't seem much deterrent of a multibillion dollar tax scam that cash flow still continues.

~~~~~~~~~~~

12. Light Touch Bank Regulation

The more I studied Ruly English the easier it became to retrace shadow banking inputs and outputs how crafty coiners convert unreal tax-credits on paper to launder paper to cash that someone else spends real money from fake tax losses through a tax loophole.

My studies took me to notice a triune system in bank workflow, dataflow, and cash flow analysis and in the bank language of business operation of a tax loophole designed to enrich a few at the cost of everyone else.

I moved away from Canada as a legal nightmare ended with a TIA – Transient Ischemic attack that dulled my senses. I went to England where I had once lived in my youth. It gave me space from psychotic lawyers.

Lawyers took care of business with another Affidavit of Subscribing Witness signed by a lawyer as agent for the bank swore witness of me signing one consent to dismiss one court action to another in a different court was okay as long as not clearing paid writs until it had signed releases— was not perceived as blackmail.

It was such a relief the bank got what it wanted while I recovered my health. I wrote my legal battles in a bank spoof called *'Contaging, the Tax Invaders Plan'*, which was published in 2011. *'Contaging'* was a big success that copies are still advertised on the internet as if still in print today. But the second edition is out in 2019, titled, *'Recontaging the Carney Mark'*.

Other than citing HRH Queen Elizabeth the Second, COMER Plaintiffs did not name Defendants. There was nothing in UK news about Mark Carney defending a lawsuit in Canada. He was touted the best candidate for next governor of the Bank of England.

I was convalescing in England when Mervyn King announced his retirement and Mark Carney appeared in the news running to be Governor of the UK Pound.

There are more newspapers in England than Canada. Features are generally more analytical and interesting. Bank of England Governor, Mervyn King was reported in the Daily Telegraph on March 5, 2011 to caution the public that banks target *'gullible clients'* for profit.

But, I had no expectation Mark Carney would testify in the COMER Action, or, that it would ever go to trial.

On March 17, 2011, Lord Turner, Chairman of FSA – Financial Services Authority was in Guardian News in a column heading warning about *'exotic'* banking;

'Lord Turner seeks eternal vigilance over banks'. The report spelled out financial consumer safeguards and need to *'regulate shadow banking to ensure new risks do not emerge outside mainstream banking'*.

Opinion was divided on a non-British Bank of England Governor that the government set up a review under the auspices of the UK Treasury Select Committee. It allowed for public input that I approached my MP, John Mann to talk about tax scams for the rich.

MP, John Mann said he appreciated my testimony and so I became a Bank Whistleblower in 2012.

English media had more coverage of criminal banking. It was in daily reports and weekend editions that kept the story alive. Lord Turner and Sir Mervyn King as he was knighted; spoke out for bank reform. So, I wrote the Parliamentary Commission on Banking Standards, to Sir John Vickers, about transparency that a bank transaction code would add safety to the system.

The Guardian | Thursday 17 March 2011

Financial

Republish License: Copyright Guardian News & Media Ltd 2011
http://www.guardian.co.uk/business/2011/mar/16/financial-services-authority-banks-regulations

Turner seeks eternal vigilance over banks

Richard Wachman

Lord Turner, chairman of the Financial services Authority, calls for strict control over banking sector's exotic activities

Lord Turner, chairman of the Financial Services Authority, warned last night that the financial system faces new risks despite the global regulatory overhaul in the wake of the banking crisis.

His words come amid renewed fears about stability in the eurozone after Moody's cut Portugal's credit rating, and analysts warned the country could follow Greece and Ireland in seeking a bailout.

Speaking at the Cass Business School in London, Turner warned against complacency, saying: "We are deluding ourselves if we think there is any one policy - one silver bullet - which will permanently ensure a more stable system."

Turner called for careful control of shadow banking - the hedge fund, derivatives and private equity industries - to ensure new risks do not emerge outside mainstream banking.

He suggested systemically important firms, the banks dubbed "too big to fail", should be required to hold more capital than new thresholds agreed by the Basel committee on banking supervision.

Turner said: "(We) should identify whether financial activities are shifting to new institutions and markets. If in response to Basel III, credit extension moves to new shadow bank markets and firms, for instance to hedge funds, and within those markets and firms we are aware of bank-like risks, such as high leverage, we need to spot that and if necessary extend the reach of regulation."

The FSA chairman stopped short of calling for the break-up of big banks by ordering them to separate their retail arms from their more risky investment banking operations. But he threw his weight behind a review of the issue by the banking commission, which is due to report in September.

Turner said the commission under Sir John Vickers should not be constrained by any assumption that the "present complex structures of banks always deliver vital social benefits - too often indeed, they reflect the objectives of tax avoidance and regulatory arbitrage." But he added that breaking up large banks might not be a panacea, since risks could also arise from the complex inter-connectedness of many small banks.

Looking at the pitfalls of future regulation of the City, Turner said the pre-crisis delusion was that the financial system was secure because risk was widely spread among scores of financial institutions. That proved to be entirely wrong.

"But the temptation post-crisis is to imagine that if we can only discover and correct the crucial imperfections - the bad incentives and structures - a permanent, more stable financial system can be achieved. It cannot, because financial instability is driven by human myopia and imperfect rationality as well as by poor incentives; and because any financial system will mutate to create new risks."

Turner said the system could be made more stable, but it required a continually evolving regulatory response. "For the very fact of imposing stricter regulations will induce changes, requiring new regulatory responses."

The FSA chairman's speech came after a turbulent day in Europe, with Moody's downgrading Portugal's credit rating to just four notches above "junk".

Sir Mervyn King, Governor of the Bank of England was alive in headline news warning banks exploit clients for bonuses that market reacted in the news;

'A fragile peace pact between the government and Britain's top banks has fractured as the Bank of England's governor, Mervyn King, delivered a scathing rebuke to top financiers for taking big bonuses while exploiting 'gullible or unsuspecting' customers.'

When the BBC – British Broadcasting Company aired Sir Mervyn's retirement speech, he admitted to having learnt from hindsight as he looked in history for bank crises, *"it is a good teacher,"* he said on television,

"With the benefit of hindsight we should have shouted from the rooftop that a system had been built in which banks were too important to fail, that banks had grown too quickly and borrowed too much, and that so-called 'light touch' regulation hadn't prevented any of this. And in the crisis we tried, but should have tried harder, to persuade every one of the need to recapitalize the bank sooner, and by more. We should have preached that the lessons of history were being forgotten, because banking crises have happened before."

There was more news about banks accused of crime and paying fines, and as Sir Mervyn King continued to explain the sector could and should have done more to prevent bankruptcies, he was quoted in the news;

'Paper fortunes in financial markets can disappear overnight.'

My life savings were lost on paper that I had to sell my house to pay lawyers who prepared my counterclaim defense, but the bank couldn't fail to collect in court, because section 165(3) is so tightly regulated.

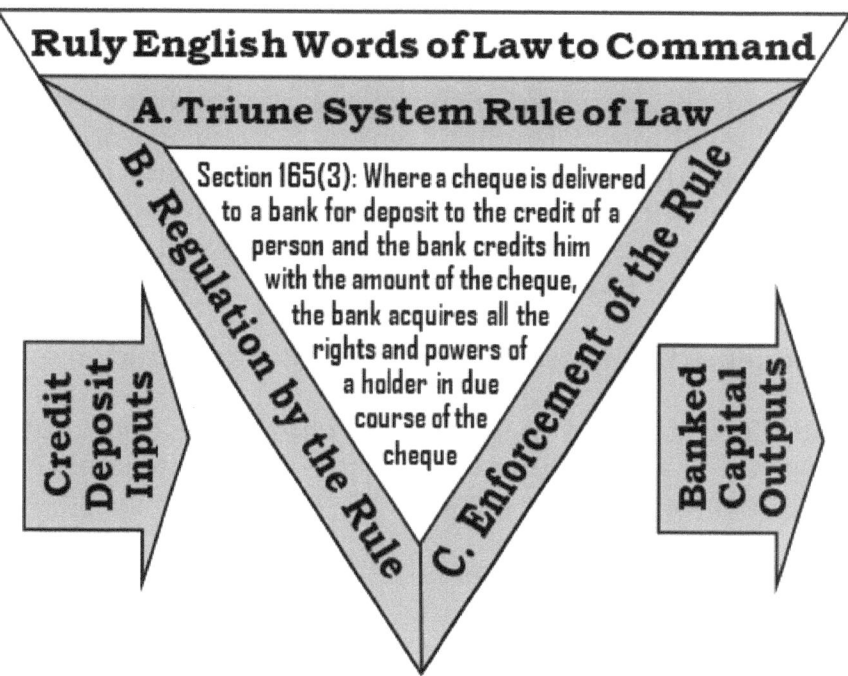

Section 165(3) is no light touch of Ruly English words of law to command rule of money in a triune system of entitlement commissioned by design.

The ABC's of A. Triune System Rule of Law involves B. Regulation by the Rule and C. Enforcement of the Rule that section 165(3) banks capital from credit deposits through chartered acquisition. It is the bank business model in the 2009 ABCP *'Crisis in Canada'* Report.

Lawyers encouraged me to write while they billed for legal words from their dictionaries and law books until I found volumes of my own from an antique bookstore in a small town in England.

Where else would you go for Ruly English books?

Bank books from the 1900s were written for people to understand banking how judges still rule today.

Case Law is defined in storybook novels of authority.

I was more interested in bank law dictionaries for the literal meaning of English, which is itself a word that means spin. When I found a Pitman's volume titled, Bills, Cheques, and Notes, it included Notes on the Law of Negotiable Instruments with Special Reference to Bills of Exchange, Promissory Notes, and Cheques.

It explained all I wanted to know but was afraid to ask.

The difference of a Ruly English charter to a computer program is remarkable that just as bank law is always right— binary code is always in contrast to legal fiction;

'Assumption that something is true even though it may be untrue, made especially in judicial reasoning to alter how a legal rule operates; specifically, device by which a legal rule or institution is diverted from its original purpose to accomplish indirectly some other object.'

The COMER Action was reported in the Toronto Star in May 2008. It was about the same time a judge ruled against me for the bank to collect a seemingly obvious forged photocopied note, which was not reported news.

The bank effect is not so much light touch regulation by the rule, as much as little enforcement of the rule.

I asked to see the original, which was refused, and not returned, even after repaid by order of the court.

That is what deregulation means. I pleaded for trial of falsified tax-credit worth for 8 years until my appeal for a hearing was denied in 2009. Similarly, COMER sued 6 years until it was denied trial in 2017.

~~~~~~~~~~~

13. Never Sign a Windbill Rule

Webster's Dictionary lookups on *'surreal'* spiked in November 2016 the day Donald Trump, himself a tax credit billionaire, not having paid income tax some 20 years, went from candidate— to US President Elect.

William Thomson defined the bank meaning of money as *'stupendous'* rather than *'surreal'* in his dictionary;

'The standard by which the value of commodities is measured, and the medium by which they are bought and sold. Money and credit, to which it gave birth, form the basis on which the stupendous business of banking has been built up. There is probably nothing which is of greater importance in the civilised world than money, and nothing which comes more closely in contact with mankind in every department of life. Not only have all conceivable commodities a monetary value attached to them, but it is customary to ascribe a financial reason as the prime moving cause (either directly or indirectly) in almost every action in which a man is concerned.'

It was more than 100 years ago that Thomson defined credit born of money, known as debt is money today. The distinction that bad debt is not good money is in the Bills of Exchange Act, 1882, which recapitalizes a Windbill in debt from one with credit to one without.

People like Thomson were more familiar with Ruly English in the Bills of Exchange Act when it was written at centuries ago. The word *'stupendous'* is a perfect word that stupefies due to the bank effect;

"Stupendous: adj. L., stupendus, amazing, especially because of size or intensity, to be struck senseless, or be amazed at, to become stupefied, F, stupéfier, cause utter consternation, bewilderment."

Thomson defined how a Windmill, or Windbill, Kites imaginary credit in Kite Flying is a Fictitious Bill, also called an Accommodation Bill, in the Act;

'A bill to which a person called an accommodation party puts his name to oblige or accommodate another person without receiving any consideration for so doing. The position of such a party is in fact, that of a surety or guarantor.'

The Windbill bank effect that converting unreal credit to real money required special treatment defined in Thomson's Banking Law and Practice published by Pitman around 1911, of which I have a copy.

The University of California Library digitized the 1911 edition of Thomson's Dictionary of Banking, by William Thomson, Bank Inspector of banking. The electronic *'Concise Encyclopedia of Banking Law and Practice'* is an excellent resource to study Ruly English. Pitman also published another volume in 1907 that defined the workings of negotiable instruments in more detail in, BILLS, CHEQUES, AND NOTES, with a subtitle, A HANDBOOK FOR LAWYERS AND BUSINESSMEN written by Barrister J. A. Slater. The guide includes a **WARNING** of financial danger especially that a banker must **NEVER SIGN A WINDBILL**.

Barrister Slater defined the Accommodation Bill in the mechanics of raising money by kite-flying like sails on a Windmill turn, today is called a Windbill;

'Never draw or accept an accommodation bill, unless you are prepared to meet it whenever called upon. After it has left your possession value may be given for it, and it is no answer to a holder for value that you are only an accommodation party.

Thomson's Dictionary of Banking and Slater's Guide for Lawyers and Businessmen have been transcribed to a web-media e-book that anyone can read the usury Ways and Means of Windbills.

BILLS, CHEQUES, AND NOTES, on the cover of this book, defines law how title of a negotiable instrument is not the same as possession of a normal chattel;

'Bills of Exchange, Cheques, and Notes, form, after coin of the realm, the most common examples of what are known as 'negotiable instruments'. There is a well-known maxim of the English common law that no person can give to another that of which he has not the true ownership "nemo dat quod non habet". This maxim applies to all ordinary chattels, and therefore no one but the rightful owner can, except as far as provision is made by statute, transfer the property, that is, the absolute ownership, in them. Negotiable instruments, however, are an exception to this rule. "A negotiable instrument," writes an eminent authority, "is one the property in which is acquired by anyone who takes it 'bona fide' and for value, notwithstanding any defect of title in the person from whom he took it; from which it follows that an instrument cannot be negotiable unless it is such and in such a state that the true owner could transfer the contract or engagement contained therein by simple delivery of the instrument." The latter part of the definition is important; the document must be complete at the time of transfer.

There are three important particulars in which negotiable instruments differ from ordinary chattels:-

(1) The property in them, that is the complete right of ownership, passes by delivery, and not merely the possession, that is, the right of retaining the same as against any person except the true owner.

(2) The holder in due course is not in any way affected by any defect of title on the part of the transferor or of any previous holder. He holds the instruments, as it is said, "free from all the equities."

(3) The holder in due course can sue upon them in his own name.

The passage continues: These are three great qualities which go to make up what is called *'negotiability'*. A rough-and-ready test of negotiability lies in a question;

'Can a title be made through a thief?'

If the answer is 'Yes' the instrument is negotiable,

If the answer is 'No' it is not negotiable.'

Thomson's Dictionary also defines negotiability with respect to a Fictitious Bill seemingly made to thieve;

'A negotiable instrument is an exception to the general rule of law that 'nemo dat quod non habet' (no one can give what he has not), a transferee can obtain good title from a thief even against the true owner.'

And, '...a transferee with notice of defect of title there must be something more than negligence.'

'...A cheque, bill, and promissory note are negotiable instruments, and the Bills of Exchange Act, 1882, provides that where a person is a holder in due course he holds the bill free from any defect of title of prior parties and may enforce payment against all parties liable on the bill. A holder in due course is a holder who takes a bill complete and regular on the face, before it is overdue, in good faith and for value and without notice of any defect in the title of the person who negotiated it.'

All the lawyers advised me follow the money, but not in the case of Windbills. The more they used and sued the law to bill me through law enforcement, the more truth there is in Bleak House, by Charles Dickens;

'The one great principle of English law is, to make business for itself.'

The modern Windbill is an old fashion Windmill used to raise unsecured credit offset in the account of an Accommodation Party signed up to pay debt in default.

Contemporary coiners of false money *'Kite'* tax-credit Windbills construed to convert public debit to private credit carried over from central bank balances to retail bank balances using double-presentment conversions technically known as, *'Rent-Seeking-Tax-Arbitrage'*.

The Windbill is defined in the Bills of Exchange Act, 1882, on the regulatory side of the legal triune system.

The enforcement side of the triune relies on judgment of money in NOTES ON THE LAW OF NEGOTIABLE INSTRUMENTS WITH SPECIAL REFERENCE TO BILLS OF EXCHANGE PROMISSORY NOTES AND CHEQUES to settle equity issues whenever pled in courts of law.

William Krehm was denied trial in May 2015, which he appealed in 2016. But, Ann Emmett seemingly lost the faith, she said on COMER video on the Internet,

"When the law doesn't work, then we have to politically change the law."

Whatever faith is lost in justice, none of it can be lost in technology and bank system analysis that I learnt Ruly English for COMER if judges allowed it in court.

~~~~~~~~~~~

Clockwise: Tony Crawford and former PM Paul Martin discuss the 1994 *'Debt Crisis in Canada'* Report and Crawford and Prof Larry Summers meet at the INET Conference in Toronto in 2014. Crawford meets Purdy Crawford to discuss twice-paid tax-credit Windbills, and Crawford and Finance Minister, James Flaherty in 2008. Crawford and Goldman Sachs CEO Gary Cohn discuss trick bank loans at G20 Conference in 2009. Crawford presents his draft Ruly English Dictionary to William Krehm and Ann Emmett in Court in 2015.

14. Front and Back Office Windbill Sales

The bank filed a system user guide in the court record. It defined an ABCP *'Acquire-to-Distribute'* business of a *shadow bank; affidavit taking, debt creating, tax credit claiming, moneymaking machine* in bank terminology.

A lawyer bought commercial real estate with a rent encumbered mortgage and applied for TS - Tax Shelter designation that the CRA granted in 1989. The bank setup *'Off-site Loans Closings'* for the lawyer as agent to operate a bank within the bank as ABCP Promoter and *'Dealer'* in a **FRONT OFFICE**, and ABCP Sponsor, *'Underwriter'* in a **BACK OFFICE** selling package deals to *'Investors'* called ABCP Asset Providers prequalified for pre-executed loans contrived to bill contingent private and public losses in a so-called *'Toxic Loans'* column;

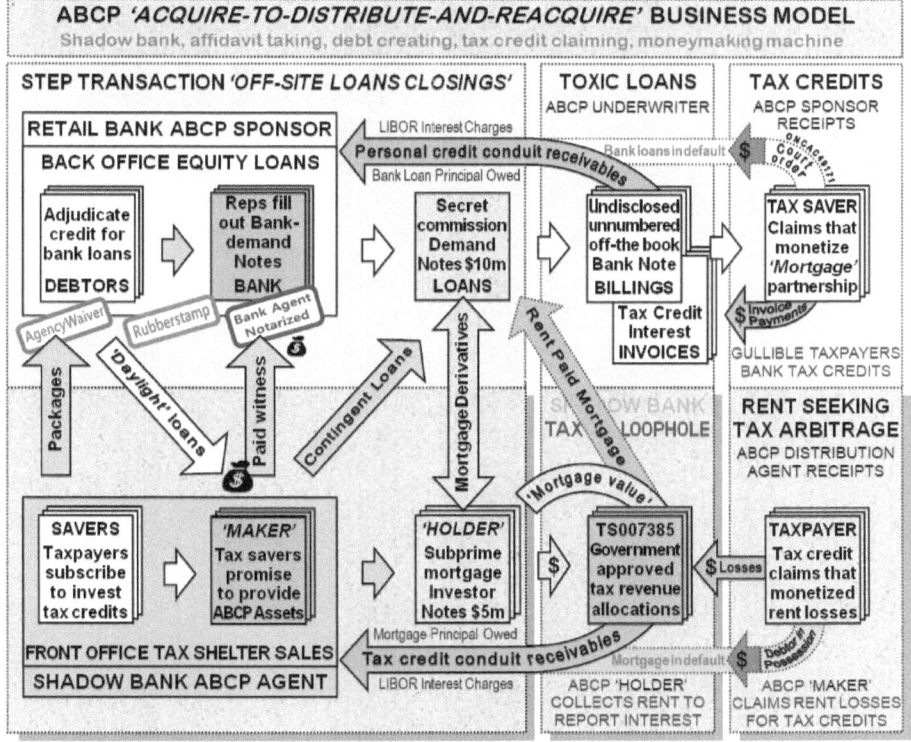

The bank defined a shadow bank agent 5-Step process how Perris sold me an ABCP Package Deal from the front office where the ABCP Dealer notarized witness sent to the ABCP Sponsor in the back office where the bank input a *'Statement of Net Worth'* that Perris filled out exaggerated net worth for a lending decision that he filled out a signed otherwise blank Demand Note for the bank to date to fund the sale and work the scam;

CANADIAN LIMITED PARTNERSHIP
HOW TO SUBSCRIBE

Please complete the following documents:

1. SUBSCRIPTION AGREEMENT
  (a) sign, witness and date page 5 and complete required information

2. INVESTOR NOTE
  (a) sign, witness and date page 4

3. STATEMENT OF NET WORTH
(for investors who are applying for 100% equity financing
  (a) complete all details listed on the Statement of Net Worth, sign and witness
  (b) you will be required to provide 2 years proof of income which should include the front page of the last 2 years Income Tax Returns including a copy of the Schedule 4 and Schedule 7 for each year if applicable. (If self-employed the bank has requested 2 years financial statements for the business)

4. LOAN DOCUMENTS
  (a) sign and witness the loan documents included in the package as indicated (**DO NOT DATE THE DEMAND NOTE** as this document must be dated on the day the funds are advanced by the bank)

5. RETURN OF DOCUMENTS
  (a) return the completed documents to our office:
    Canadian Equities Corporation
    207 Queen's Quay West
    Suit 450, P.O. Box 112
    Toronto, Ontario M5J 1A7
If you require any assistance, please contact our office at 360-0212

The back office bank had its own checklist to validate package deals as they came in from the front office.

The retail bank checklist ensured the legality of the ABCP package including; *'Subscription Agreement'*, *'Investor Note'*, and *'Agency Waiver'*, signed, witnessed and dated, a *'Statement of Net Worth'* filled out signed and dated, *'Affidavit of Subscribing Witness'*, signed, dated, notarized, and the all-important *'Demand Note'*;

'DO NOT DATE THE DEMAND NOTE *as this document must be dated on the day the funds are advanced by the bank.*

Bank *'Demand Note'* completion started with the bank logo rubberstamped in the top-left and bank name written in the payee line of an inchoate note.

The bank transcribed *'Statement of Net Worth'* from Perris to its CCAP – Central Credit Approval Process to assess my creditworthy as a taxpayer to carry a bank loan in the works of a government approved tax-saver scheme in the same person name of an *'Investor Note'* at my expense as a taxpayer, as well as a tax-saver.

That was the object of tax-deductible securities fraud.

The ABCP Distribution Agent gathered signatures for the ABCP Sponsor in the *'Acquire-to-Distribute'* model that a taxpayer signed a promise as the tax-saver and ABCP Asset Provider in the *'Subscription Agreement'*.

That was the purpose of a tax-credit ABCP Windbill.

The next step was the bank-lending decision advised to Perris as paid witness to tax-shelter deal to fill out the *'Demand Note'* amount for a *'Daylight Loan'*;

'the sole purpose of completing interconnected financial transactions that must be processed all on the same business day for legal reasons.'

That was the purpose of the bank technology.

The success of the fraud depended on nondisclosure that the tax-credit ABCP Windbill *'Maker'* never knew the ABCP Sponsor paid its ABCP Distribution Agent to close sales, or that the ABCP Windbill *'Holder'* was in receipt of tax-credit *'like'* money in acceptance whereof debt to charge interest on principal— also to collect.

Bank technology was complicated enough that while workflow, dataflow, and cash flow was easy for me to follow, regulatory arbitrage was not. It is an entirely different thing; it is a doctrine in the practice of law.

Perris had the advantage of being a trained accountant taught in crafty ways of banking. Mine was an ordeal of reflection in self-study and doubt. No one confirmed or denied what I learnt and wrote about a Windbill.

Indeed, the bank denied it existed to avoid trial.

When the TS00385 deal closed on December 1, 1989 it conveyed near $5m in tax-credit Investor Notes to an ABCP Distribution Agent mortgage account and $10m in ABCP Sponsor Demand Notes into an unnumbered financial conduit geared to channel ABCP Provider tax-credit savings into bank profits.

The scandal of unregulated shadow banking behind tax-deductible securities fraud was framed as though regulated inside normal commercial bank operations. Which is the very reason Sir Mervyn King supported Sir John Vickers to *'ring fence'* commercial banking separate from investment banking layers shown in the ABCP *'Acquire-to-Distribute'* business model. Each deal conjured mortgage derived make-believe tax-credit ABCP Windbill value to perform *'like'* money in both private and public financial markets at the same time.

None of ABCP in my name could have been sold to defraud any other way. But it was not proven in court.

The authorities developed a vernacular in general the public only heard of *'toxic loans'* and *'exotic assets'* in review of the ABCP *'Crisis in Canada'*.

The 2009 ABCP *'Crisis in Canada'* Report was more definitive about ABCP Assets and ABCP Loans. When I met Finance Minister, James Flaherty he understood my concern and he agreed unnumbered loans should be tracked with transaction control numbers, he said,

"It will help our tax authorities enforce tax laws and combat tax evasion."

Hindsight pictured my tax credits in 3 columns: ABCP Assets in one column for *'Off-Site Loans Closings'*, and an SIV in the second column for *'Toxic Loans'*, and tax claims in a third column for *'Tax Credits'* hidden from the Treasury not reported in the budget, which is what COMER claimed was breached in constitutional law.

The underwriting bank set up SIV *'Toxic Loans'* with *'Undisclosed unnumbered off-the book personal loans'* in *'Billings'* that issued tax credit interest *'Invoices'* for the gullible taxpayer to bank tax credits as deposits into *'Personal Credit Conduit Receivables'* in response to the retail bank billing the *'Mortgage Partnership'*.

Billings continued while; the ABCP Distribution Agent collected his *'Rent Paid Mortgage'* in the bank effect of *'Government approved tax revenue allocations'* paid in to *'Tax credit conduit receivables'*.

Perris was my accountant all the years he prepared my business and personal tax returns over the 10 year ABCP subprime mortgage term.

ABCP Sponsor and ABCP Distribution Agent contrived ABCP tax receipts that I paid ABCP mortgage interest through taxation before its principal fell in default.

I had absolutely no idea I was part of a tax scam.

I didn't see it even when the CRA audited my business and personal taxes twice in 6 years while I continued to save my income tax credits into personal financial ruin and notional national debt. I only figured it out when the bank sued a photocopy of a *'Demand Note'* filled out by Perris to collect. The bank showed me his signed sworn witness of me being the same person as one who signed an *'Investor Note'*, which the bank lied in court— the lawyer said it didn't exist to avoid trial.

But it was already counted in audits to re-tax income.

In the credit event of the subprime mortgage failure to rollover in default the ABCP Sponsor bank won a court order to collect principal debt without trial. And, the ABCP Distribution Agent collected *'Mortgage value'* as the *'DIP – Debtor in Possession'* took my CDS payment in final disbursements in settlement of full account of *'Tax Savers promise to provide ABCP Assets'*.

The ABCP *'Crisis in Canada'* Report figured hundreds of billions of dollars lost to ABCP *'Third Party Notes'*.

Lawyers said I was a poor loser to a bad investment decision that I was responsible as a victim of my own misfortune. The lawyer for the bank said I had made up a conspiracy theory to avoid my responsibility to pay what the bank claimed I had borrowed to invest.

It was certainly not something I had in legalese to explain tax-deductible fraud to an unbelieving judge.

~~~~~~~~~~~

15. Twice Paid Tax Credit Windbill Posters

When judges ruled no issue in bank documentation for trial it separated bank workflow and data analysis from cash flow at the business analysis end of debt in *'Rent Seeking Tax Arbitrage'* tax shelter schemes.

A *'Double-Presentment'* Twice-Paid-Tax-Credit-Windbill in the big picture centered on a secret circle of cash flow in the ABCP *'Acquire-to-Distribute'* business model defined in the 2009 ABCP *'Crisis in Canada'* Report.

ABCP sales spanned a few months for Perris to target high income earners for his enablers to commandeer personal wealth of gullible taxpayers in a sleazy storybook tax shelter scheme. Once the trap was set in the *'Acquire-to-Distribute'* business model— to recycle debt through mortgage term until sub-primes failed to rollover in default, years on, sometimes decades later.

It depended on what the industry called repackaging, which in banking is a euphemism for resold debt.

When the court ruled against trial of a Demand Note to a bank forged in my name it ruled out counterclaim against; Perris, the ABCP Rep, the bank, the ABCP Sponsor, and tax shelter promoter, ABCP Distribution Agent. A judge saved the bank that freed its agent and Perris from trial of contingent debt forged in my name.

The ABCP *'Acquire-to-Distribute'* business model set up unnumbered tax savings loan accounts in a *'Conduit'* that the ABCP Sponsor billed the same interest rate as the underlying mortgage that as a gullible taxpayer, and thinking of myself as a tax-saver I claimed income tax-credits issued by the government to invest.

I never thought it was a tax scam for the rich.

The ABCP Distribution Agent, ABCP Property Owner collected rent accounted as tax-credit Windbill interest on mortgage principal as *'Rent Seeking Tax Arbitrage'* routed public losses into private profits in my name.

I had unwittingly signed an ABCP Windbill negotiable instrument that my tax-credits circulated *'like'* money in private and public markets at the same time until the subprime mortgage on property sold as an investment failed in default of a debt crisis in my name.

Double presentment started with ABCP Sponsor bank-paid witnessing of *'Signature-Specific-Identity-Theft'* for unsigned, unacknowledged, secret commission bank loans tied to sales. Cash flowed through mortgages until failures in default triggered private and public losses, either repaid on account, or sued to collect.

2009 ABCP *'Crisis in Canada'* Report

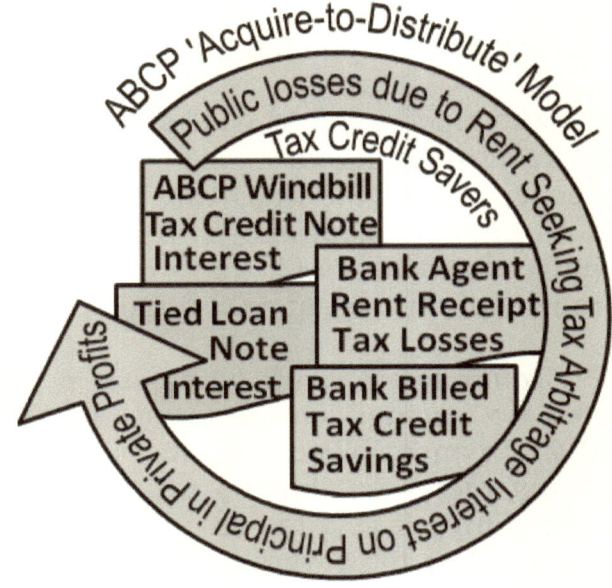

Subprime mortgage failures to rollover converged in mass in 2008 when duped tax-credit savers were held responsible for CDO – Collateralized Debt Obligations.

CDO debts were settled in ❶ ❷ ❸ Step Transactions.

Double Presentment Twice Paid Tax Credit Windbill Principal

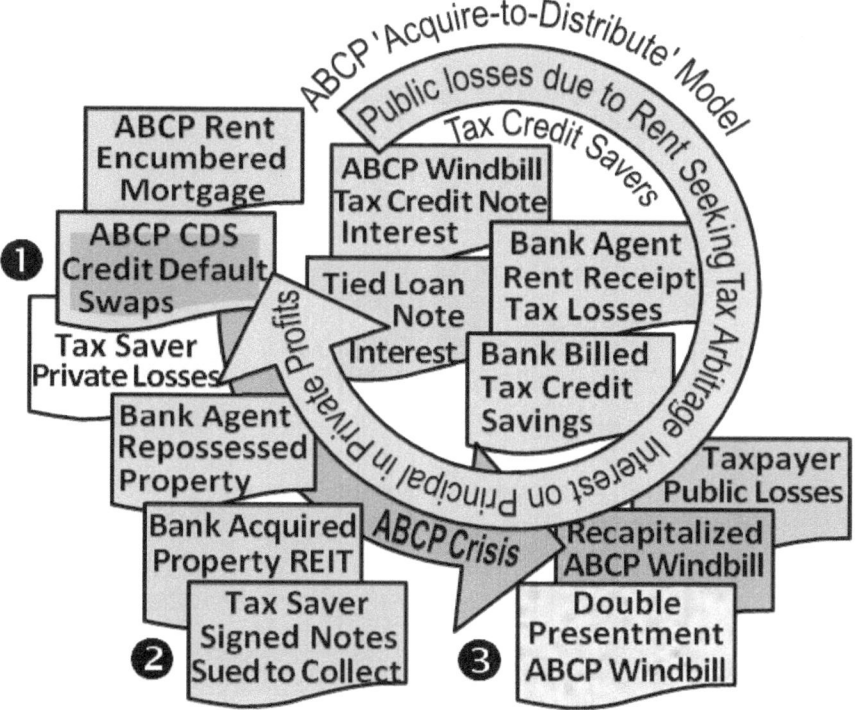

❶ The first ABCP CDO repaid mortgage principal that all CDS – Credit Default Swaps were accounted as tax-saver private losses that the mortgage on property sold as a tax sheltered investment in 1998 was paid to the ABCP Promoter as DIP – Debtor in Possession in 2002.

The ABCP Sponsor bank acquired ABCP Promoter real estate resold in a REIT – Real Estate Investment Trust offered in bank Capital Markets in 2003 while it was still managed by the ABCP Distribution Agent.

❷ The second CDO paid tax-saver Demand Notes that the ABCP Sponsor sued to collect the balance of loans.

❸ The third CDO paid ABCP that as a tax-credit saver having paid ❶ CDS private losses also identified by the ABCP Sponsor paid witness and notarized by its ABCP Agent to be the same person identified in my name as a taxpayer liable to pay an ABCP Windbill in dishonor through a double presented public loss— twice over.

My step-transaction analysis was not welcome in court that it was ruled inadmissible as just not credible, but also contrary to traditional economic theory, which is not actually regarded as a pure science.

Others wanted to see my bank system analysis.

I was invited to prepare a poster presentation for the University of Zurich FINEXUS Conference in 2018 that I made an art rendition of the *'Magna Carta Loophole'*.

Poster presentations were new to me that I struggled with the artistic format. But I was surprised how many people stopped to talk about bank system design in a poster for criminally minded confidence tricksters.

The Magna Carta Loophole emerged from what lawyers said in COMER hearings that my presentation poster included a shadow banking top-layer of magnetized grey symbols that peeled away to reveal a color-coded commercial bank layer underneath. It demonstrated the need for taxpayer protection in context of a quote by renowned economist, John Maynard Keynes,

'I work for government I despise for ends I think criminal.' [7]

---

[7] John Maynard Keynes letter to Duncan Grant in 1917

The poster advertised my work that had compiled a Crawford's Pocket Money to Ruly English Dictionary;

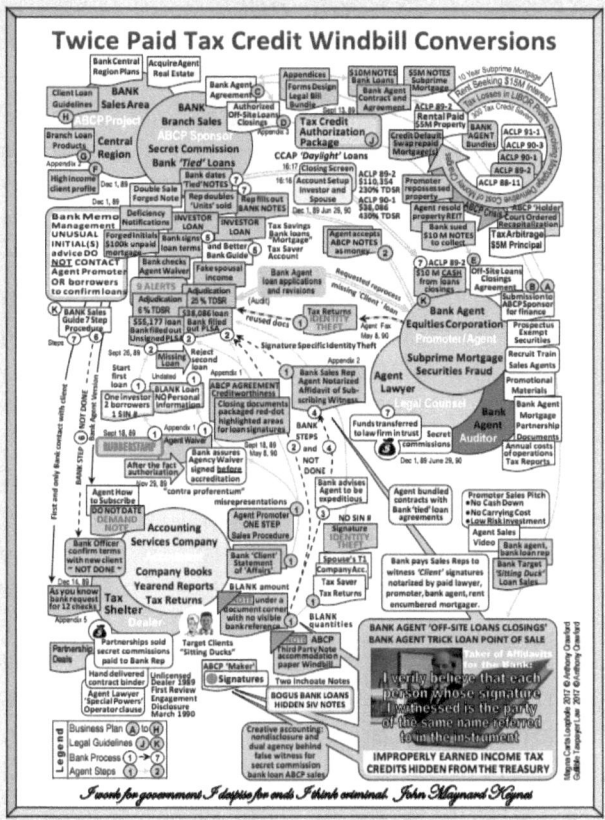

The 1215 Magna Carta Loophole was established in the Bank of England behind the first deficit economy in the world in 1694. It was discovered in 2017 when the Supreme Court of Canada ruled Canadian taxpayers must complain about it to their representatives. Tony Crawford presented this work of art to the Finance Committee for their review in the 2017 Tax Plan that without bank transaction numbers people need more protection than tax codes provide.

 Crawford's Pocket Money to English Dictionary
Gullible Taxpayer Law Edition 2018
University of Zurich FINEXUS Conference January 17, 2018

I included an introduction to explain the accounting problem of unnumbered bank notes in system design;

'The 1215 Magna Carta Loophole was established in the Bank of England behind the first deficit economy in the world in 1694. It was discovered in 2017 when the Supreme Court of Canada ruled Canadian taxpayers must complain about it to their representatives. Tony Crawford presented this work of art to the Finance Committee for their review in the 2017 Tax Plan that without a bank transaction number people need more protection than tax code provides.'

The way that judges refused to look beyond Perris and his trick ABCP loans made me think of the timeline to defraud. Each ❶ ❷ ❸ bank-step-transaction put time between so-called credit events, which not numbered seemed unrelated, even separate from each other.

There was no bank transaction number on imaginary credit used in 1990 that my unnumbered bank loan was hidden from its credit rating; otherwise it could, and should, have warned me of theft in my name.

There was no bank transaction number to connect the tax-shelter property subprime mortgage repossessed in 1999 as a contingent liability to a 1989 mortgage term bank loan— sued to collect in 2002, repaid in 2012.

And there was no bank transaction number to link me, a tax saver signing a tax-credit Note as its *'Maker'* in 1989, to me a taxpayer liable to pay the *'Holder'* of the original tax-credit Note in *'Due Course'* in 2012.

People thanked me for my poster and wanted to know if the Court had changed the law to close the loophole.

All I could say, Galati appealed for trial of the budget,

"The other part... which goes hand-in-hand with this whole banking fraud that's going on is against the Minister of Finance and the budgetary process."

There were about a dozen poster presentations in the concourse where conference organizers set up tables for luncheon. People had leisure time to review posters in a great setting for conversation. The concourse led to practitioner sessions where speakers were grouped by topics with a chairperson who facilitated discussion and fielded questions from the audience.

I was interested in a Central Bank session, and I had a question in context of my poster presentation,

"Yesterday I spoke with regards to a concept in Canada where Canadian taxpayers sued the Minister of Finance for a trillion dollars with respect to the case of the Bank of Canada being a Public Bank owned by the people giving loans which are basically interest free. And, they saw the danger of that being taken away from them"

I mentioned my request for a Private Members Bill,

"Currently, this question is before Parliament with a request for a Private Members Bill to keep the Bank of Canada a Public Bank. And, Justice Russell through the Supreme Court and Federal Court of Canada has engaged every taxpayer to complain to their Members of Parliament to see that the bill is passed for the reason that it cannot go to Court. It will not be allowed in Court. So, it's a burning question and I am glad you asked me to put it forward. And I would like our panel to comment on the capability of a Public Bank verses a Private Bank being a Central Bank."

Alexander Barkawi, Director, Council on Economic Policies hedged the answer,

"Forgive me if I kind of duck the question, because I think a) I am not knowledgeable enough to answer it, and b) it would be a very long conversation. Maybe just a few thoughts, I think there are successful examples of different governance structures in Central Banking."

He referenced the FINEXUS conference and back to what they had said in the Central Bank session,

"José Manuel you alluded to the fact that the Swiss Central Bank for example is a listed company, obviously the government holds the majority especially in decision making, and the ECB has a completely different setup. So, I'm not sure whether that is a dichotomy that is leading in one way, or the other. I think at the end-of-the-day it comes down to accountability, processes, transparency, etcetera, and my gut feeling is you can probably structure these things with both forms of governance, like as legal forms."

José Manuel Marques, Head of International Finance Markets Division, Banco de España agreed,

"I agree with Alexander, I think that the most important is the designs of the accountability, transparency, this kind of thing are important. The structure of the Central Bank is different, it depends on historical reasons, the Federal Structure, and sometimes it is difficult to change because of these sensibilities that are among residents of your countries. We have no evidence of this, it is clearly what is important. What is important is really; what is your structure? What is your level of independence? How do you report? What is your accountability? What is your transparency? How clear is the independence mandated in the validity of independence of the Central Banks?"

~~~~~~~~~~~

16. Don Quixote Tilts at Windbills

Talk show host Richard Syrett from Toronto affiliate AM 640 Radio dedicated a show to the COMER affair, [8]

"...a most important case before the Federal Courts here in Canada... and it's largely being ignored by the mainstream media in Canada. This Bank of Canada was created by an Act of Parliament. And, its raison d'etre, its reason for existence, was to lend money interest free, that's right, interest free to the Federal, Provincial, and Municipal governments in this country..."

"Again, zero interest, this is how Canada paid for the war effort, during the Second World War. It's how we paid for one of the most important infrastructure projects in our history, the Saint Lawrence Seaway. It's how we paid for universal healthcare, again, interest free, from the Bank of Canada. Then, in the early to the mid-1970's something changed, the federal government here in Canada stopped borrowing interest free money from the Bank of Canada, and instead we went to the international money market, we started borrowing from international lenders and paying interest. Now today, in 2016, the Federal debt, here in Canada, is about $600 billion, and most of that, probably about 80, 90 percent of that, is compound interest from the loans from international lenders."

"Why is this happening, when we have the Bank of Canada Act? My guest in the first two hours of Coasttocoast is a constitutional lawyer who's alleging a conspiracy on the part of the Bank of Canada, and various Finance Ministers, and, no less the Queen of England. This is not just a Canadian story; it has serious implications for countries around the world..."

---

[8] https://www.coasttocoastam.com/show/2016/02/14

"Again... in the United States we have the Federal Reserve Bank; the various countries in Europe have their Central Banks. As this court case gets to the very core of how our economies are being controlled, perhaps at the very top, anyway Canadian constitutional lawyer Rocco Galati is standing by... stay with us..."

Syrett introduced Rocco Gallati to millions of listeners,

"Welcome... Rocco Galati is an Italian born Canadian lawyer, who specializes in cases involving constitutional law... He is currently pursuing a case against the Canadian government to restore the original intended use of the Bank of Canada as a lender to government."

'Welcome to Coasttocoastam, how are you?"

"Good morning Richard, I'm a bit tired, it's one o'clock."

"Haha, well I appreciate your time, because this is an important case, and I want our American listeners, and Canadian listeners to understand the importance here."

"Just take a few moments to explain what the Bank of Canada is as it relates for example to the Federal Reserve Bank in the United States and the various Central Banks of Europe."

"Well it serves the same function as the other central banks with a huge difference..."

"Canada is the only Western Democracy in Europe and North America that has a Public Central Bank. That is the bank is owned by the public through the Minister of Finance and reports and is responsible for reporting to Parliament. The other central banks, such as the Federal Reserve, Bank of England, the Bank of Italy, and so forth, are private banks..."

"Although they have the aura, and you know, most people think they're public banks, they are not, they are private banks. So, in so far as Canada is concerned, our Public Bank has been drawn into the dictates of private bankers... We are dictated to our Public Bank not only on interest rate policy, but how it's to function, and really, er turn on its head the reason it was set up in the first place..."

Galati described reason for the Bank of Canada,

"...which was to get us out of the depression. And, to extend low interest and interest free loans to the government for human infrastructure projects, such as the hospitals, education, roads, and other government infrastructure."

Syrett reminded people of its history,

"So, the Bank of Canada was established, in fact it was nationalized by Prime Minister William Lyon Mackenzie King in 1937... to lend money to the various levels of government at essentially zero interest, is that correct?"

Galati described the sequence of events,

"Yes, that's correct, yea, and it worked for a long time. Canada far outperformed the other countries in terms of fiscal policies and economic output from the '34, to '74."

"And then in 1974, Prime Minister, Pierre Elliot Trudeau was convinced to join, what they call the Bank of International Settlements over in Basle Switzerland, which was the bank that was responsible for the post Marshall Plan reconstruction of Europe, which was the inter-committee of Central Banks. He later indicated that he regretted having made that decision, because he didn't really know enough about economics..."

"...when he made it... He was a nationalist... so he regretted his decision, because he didn't understand the impact. The impact being that private actors, private bankers are making decisions that have nothing to do with your country. They only serve the interests of their private profit making, er, you know banking operations. Yet, they determine your banking policy, which in turn determines your economic policy, which in turn takes away your sovereignty."

Syrett summarized the account,

"So, round 1974, instead of the Federal government, here in Canada, the Provincial governments, Municipal governments borrowing interest free money from the Bank of Canada, which is owned by the people of Canada, we start to borrow from international bankers, you mentioned the Bank of International Settlements."

Galati was matter of fact,

"...we also borrow from domestic banks too. The irony there is that the banks... those private banks do get their money from the Bank of Canada at next to zero interest rates, right now I think the prime rate of the Bank of Canada is half of one percent, and they in turn lend it to the government from anywhere three-and-half to four percent."

He calculated the loss at some $2 <u>trillion</u>,

"So since 1974, we have paid approximately one point seven or eight trillion dollars in interest alone. One point seven trillion in interest..."

And the lawyer gave a quick example,

"Which just to put it in perspective, our annual budget is approximately, anywhere from two-thirty to two-forty a year, so, even if you round it off to a quarter trillion dollars, you are talking about seven years of running the country. That's a lot of money..."

Syrett was concerned to ask more about COMER,

"To say the least! Now what about the case?"

Galati became the lawyer again,

"...it's taking place in Toronto, but it's been stuck almost in a, sort of a tornado, it's spinning in a procedural legal quagmire because obviously the government does not want this thing going to trial. So, there was a series, there was a series of appeals on the... on initial motion to strike the whole thing. Where we lost at the first level, won at the second level, and then both sides appealed to the Federal Court of Appeal, and both Appeals were dismissed, so essentially it went back. It went back, and then there was another round of Appeal, sorry, Motion to Strike, which was granted, which is now under appeal going back to the Federal Court of Appeal. So it's been stuck in this procedural nightmare for about four and half years."

The radio host went back to the politics of banking,

"...And, previously we had a Conservative government here in Canada, now we have a Liberal government... it doesn't seem to matter though, does it"

Galati was amused at the opportunity in the interview to compare politics to sport,

"...No, no, governments in North America aren't really governments, as we historically have known them."

"They are like different football teams with different colored jerseys; the game is the same... Er, you'd be delusional if you think one government's going to effectively act differently from another. In fact, when this Prime Minister on a campaign trail was asked of what he thought of the Bank of Canada challenge, he turned to the cameras and without knowing the first thing about it, simply said, 'Oh, I don't believe in conspiracy theories'. I don't know what that's supposed to have meant, but obviously he was not briefed on it, he didn't understand it, and I don't know how many members of his government understand it."

Syrett was quizzical about politics in succession,

"This is the current Canadian Prime Minister, the Liberal Prime Minister Justin Trudeau, whose father Pierre Elliot Trudeau was the one that essentially undermined the Bank of Canada Act..."

Galati said what happened had been a mistake,

"Yes, and to his credit though, he recognized that later in life... he was no longer Prime Minister, but he recognized that he'd made a huge mistake in doing that."

The Canadian talk show host returned to meaning,

"So, you're essentially alleging... that this is an act of treason, can I say that?"

"...essentially, yes, they have relinquished sovereignty. They have handed off sovereignty to private individuals some people see that as a form of treason. It's a very serious thing. There's, we have a constitutional doctrine that says the government cannot abdicate its duty to rule, so in that sense they've handed over the country to private individuals."

I'm a great fan of Coasttocoast and the show inspired me to write Prime Minister Trudeau about Windbills... the very next day;

Prime Minister, Hon Justin Trudeau
Office of the Prime Minister
80 Wellington Street, Ottawa, ON, K1A 0A2

February 16, 2016

Dear Prime Minister, Justin Trudeau,

Subject: Election Promise re Tax Scams for the Rich
Ref: Pre-budget Consultations Letter of February 10, 2016. File 2016FIN431315

I write about your 2015 election promise about tax scams for the rich. Minister of Finance, Hon Bill Morneau has not acknowledged receipt of my testimony how tax scams work.

Instead, his department implies I am not a tax stakeholder, and I receive repeated advice to go to a Fin-Webpage, which I have done. So, now I resend my *'Private Information'* a third time that my treatise may be confirmed, or denied.

When I met past Finance Minister, Hon James Flaherty about *'Signature-Specific-Identity-Theft'* loans in the $32 billion largest bankruptcy bailout of a financial conduit in Canadian history, he promised me Canada would criminalize identity theft. We discussed the $117 billion Capital Market collapse of CDS Credit Default Swap insured ABCP Asset Backed Commercial Paper Third Party Notes. He announced new regulation from the ABCP *'Crisis in Canada'* government report by Professor John Chant.

I am old enough with Victorian English to understand how the ABCP tax loophole expands the money supply. According to the Bills of Exchange Act, 1882, and its Notes of Law circa 1907, ABCP appears to be the *'Windbill Tax Credit Windfall'* opposite of UK budget purely financial *'Invisible Earnings'.* When you follow tax-credit promises received, people see how ABCP streams public revenue shortfalls into private profits that Professor Larry Summers defines as *'Rent Seeking Tax Arbitrage'.*

The former US Secretary of the Treasury quantifies such loss in hundreds of billions of tax dollars not collected by world fiscs, and he describes profits by government rules of law being, as he says, *"the dark side of capital".*

In my experience, judges do not ponder the wisdom of policy in laws they uphold, however outdated, or unfair, or even when, or, especially when court rulings cause financial harm. Modern tax arbitrageurs use ancient Windbill law to profit from gullible taxpayers tricked to unwittingly sign mortgage term tax-credit Accommodation Notes.

> Prime Minister, I reported how tax scams work for the rich and I petitioned for a Bill to debate the issue back in 2005. The crash was 2008. The ABCP *'Acquire-to-Distribute' business model* was not defined until 2009. Political will about tax scams was not until late 2015. I do hereby reaffirm;
>
> *"A bank transaction control number will safeguard financial consumers and protect taxpayers and the economy from ongoing multi-billion dollar rip-offs that the Treasury pays public tax revenue to the private profiteer."*
>
> **Please reply to my concern: If tax-loophole credit/debits do not count in Treasury books of accounts, how do Members of Parliament know how much tax scams cost to be able to vote for a balanced budget?**
>
> Yours truly,
>
> Anthony Crawford

As I listened to Galati on American radio I knew it was pointless of me chasing unanswered pleadings. All my letters had been ignored; so the struggle would continue as I heard Syrett ask Galati, *"Are you like Don Quixote, trying to tilt windmills?"*

Galati mentioned he had read Don Quixote, but he said it wasn't the same thing...

But to me Quixote is a cautionary tale, and it seemed to have quite a lot in common with socioeconomics. The author, Cervantes, gave a mad knight errant good reason to challenge windmills, which he cleverly wove into a modern-day story, well-ahead of its time;

"There's not a gentleman's antechamber," said Samson, "in which you will not find a Don Quixote. When one lays it down, another picks up; some rush at it; others beg for it. In fact this story is the most delightful and least harmful entertainment ever seen to this day, for nowhere in it is to be found anything even resembling an indelicate expression or an un-catholic thought."

"To write it any other way," said Don Quixote, "would be to write not the truth, but lies; and historians who resort to lies ought to be burnt like coiners of false money. My conclusion is, Master Bachelor, that to compose histories or books of any sort at all you need good judgment and ripe understanding."

Adding perceptively, *"To be witty and write humorously require great genius."*

Cervantes' genius popularized Quixote as if copied and translated in languages crafted in the story in 1604, which was reviewed by Samuel Johnson in 1786;

'Was there ever yet anything written by mere man that was wished longer by its readers, excepting Don Quixote, Robinson Crusoe, and the Pilgrim's Progress?'

The only way for me to live the illusion of delusion was to pretend madness that I billed Robby Ducky as my own hero. He was not a mad knight tilting Windmills in the *'Tax Invaders Plan'* in my bankbook story. My hero was a repentant computer geek and convenient idiot to bankers. Robby Ducky set out to flip Windbills that turned a tax-credit dollar at unwitting expense of a shrinking middleclass.

I tried to call Coasttocoastam with a question, but all lines were busy in a huge backlog of interest. It was an outstanding interview about the Bank of Canada and money that had me to write my Prime Minister, again.

The last time I spoke on Coasttocoastam was in 2007.

I had called the inimitable Art Bell. The show was also about money, and we spoke about the constitutional challenge, what people can do to change the law.

~~~~~~~~~~~

Clockwise: MP Bonnie Brown Federal Election 2006. Crawford campaign Petition 44 for NDP Leader Jack Layton 2007. MPP Andrea Horwath read Petition 44 in 2009. Crawford and Krehm at Federal Court in 2013. Galati describes budget process and Crawford speaks to bank-law dictionary at COMER Conference in 2015. Comer Claimant-Plaintiff-Appellant Erick Bittschwam Motion to Reconsider judgment in 2016. Crawford and Krehm review decision to deny trial in 2017.

17. Capitalism without Capital Ponzi

Computer programmers use workflow charts to map data processing to control operations in binary code. It is a professional skill that my diagram of the ABCP *'Acquire-to-Distribute'* model defined securities fraud from the 2009 ABCP *'Crisis in Canada'* Report.

The report labeled bank roles and procedures which I arranged in color-code order of workflow symbols and financial entities and bank loan documents connected with numbered arrows in the scope of bank design.

No one has ever criticized my analysis of bank system design in error, or my research conclusions wrong.

Just taboo that no one will take it to peer review.

Workflow complexity can be too much for most people wanting a quick overview in a business chart, which in the simple case is a Ponzi pyramid chart named after Charles Ponzi convicted in Boston in the 1920s;

'A fraudulent investment scheme geared that money from subsequent investors generates artificially high dividends to original investors.'

The amazing workings of 21st century Ponzi is that it generates interest on counterfeit tax-credit fake money that cons recapitalize illiquid assets through taxation, even in collapse by way of criminal conversion;

'The wrongful possession or disposition of another's property as if it were one's own; an act or series of acts of willful interference, without lawful justification' with any chattel in a manner inconsistent with another's right, whereby that other person is deprived of the use and possession of the chattel.'

I drew Ponzi charts for a TJN – Tax Justice Network, PowerPoint presentation at Essex University in 2011. It was on the cover of Bank Whistleblower Testimony for the UK Treasury Select Committee in 2012.

ABCP generated Ponzi cash flow from LIBOR interest cost of Bank Tied Loan Notes and subprime mortgage principal ABCP Notes until mass failures in default.

'ABCP Rent Seeking Ponzi Distributions' paid interest through Tax System Conduits that income tax credits counted in retail and shadow bank balances offset to *'Income Tax Shortfalls'* at government expense until *'ABCP Tax Arbitrage Ponzi Collections'* repaid mortgage and loan principals triggered in default.

ABCP Rent Seeking Ponzi Distributions

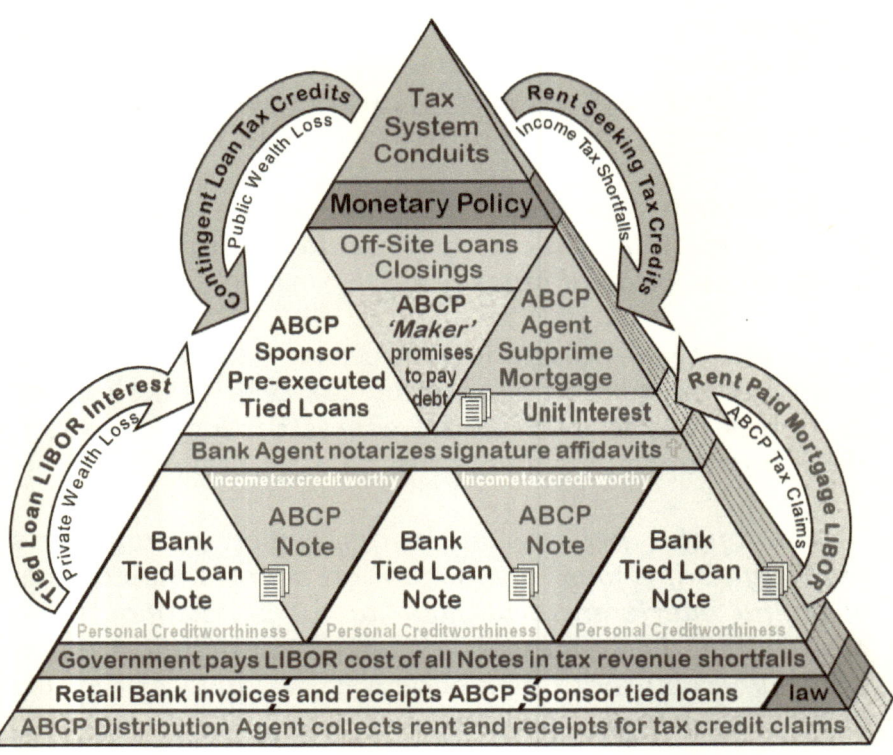

Mortgage derivatives package tacit hypothecation;

'To pledge (property) as security or collateral without delivery of title or possession,' contrived to lien in law;

'A type of lien or mortgage that is created by operation of law and without the parties' express agreement.'

Tax Shelter claims for Rent Seeking Tax Credits offset Rent Paid Mortgage LIBOR interest cost of derivative debt for an ABCP Agent Subprime Mortgage accepted *'like'* money, and Contingent Loan Tax Credits for the Tied Loan LIBOR Interest cost of undisclosed retail bank lending decisions invoiced as if a mortgage concealed ABCP Sponsor Pre-executed Tied Loans.

ABCP Tax Arbitrage Ponzi Collections

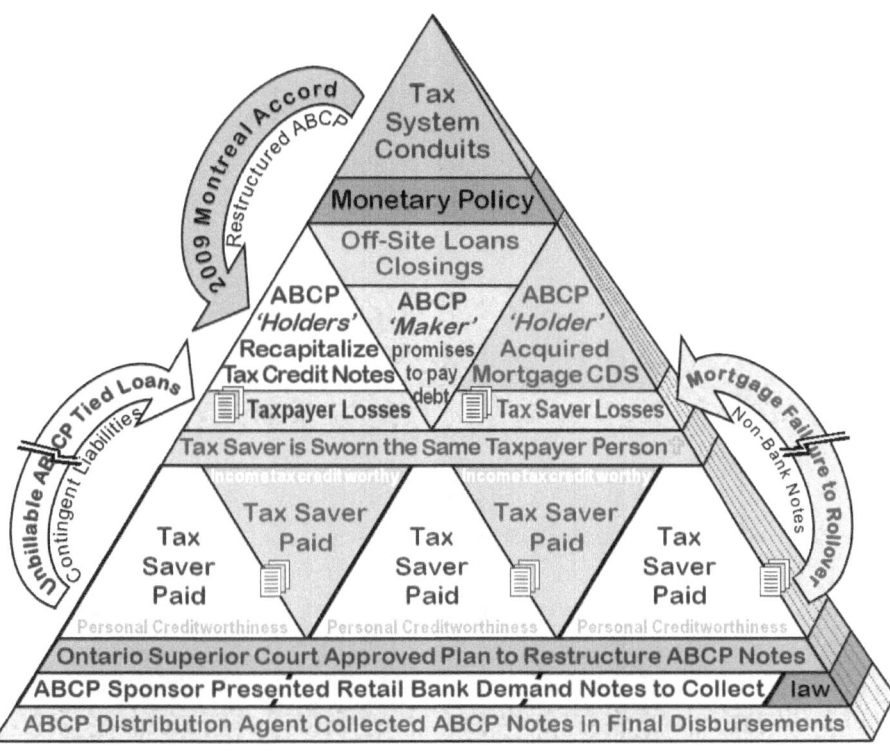

The *'Credit Event'* trigged ❶ ❷ ❸ contingent liabilities as a Tax Saver is Sworn the Same Taxpayer Person in the Ponzi *'Signature-Specific-Identity-Theft'* part used to pass-off Tax Saver Losses and Taxpayer Losses in *'Double Presentment'* of tax credits owed twice over;

First: the shadow bank effect ❶ of a rent encumbered *'Mortgage Failure to Rollover'* in default collects CDS paid to the ABCP Holder Acquired Mortgage CDS from *'Tax Saver Losses'*. In my case, the ABCP Distribution Agent collected ABCP Notes in Final Disbursements paid out of 1989 Tax Shelter CRA Number TS007385, which was dissolved in 1999.

Second: the retail bank effect ❷ of *'financial seizure'* of Unbillable ABCP Tied Loans. The underwriter could no longer invoice loans as tax shelter mortgage interest charges, which was when people found they had been tricked into debt. ABCP Sponsors positioned people as sophisticated investors in debt to investment loans with only speculation in the market to blame. If people didn't pay lending banks, they were sued to settle by summary judgment for lenders to collect in the Ponzi bottom line of ABCP Sponsor Presented Retail Bank Demand Notes to Collect.

Third: taxpayers repaid Non-Bank Notes in ❸ a general acceptance banks are considered *'too-big-to-fail'*.

I met people in banks in Europe who recognized CCAP *'Setup'* and *'Loan Closings Screens'* that it seemed to me they all used an integrated bank technology to sell tied-loan ABCP, the same as Perris did in Canada.

President Trump described the effect in basic terms,

"The wealth of our middleclass has been ripped from their homes and distributed all across the world."

My experience in court was long enough to see both private and public losses how conversion coins paper through the section 165(3) loophole;

'An ambiguity, omission, or exemption (as in law or other legal document) that provides a way to avoid a rule without violating its literal requirements; especially, a tax-code provision that allows a taxpayer to legally avoid or reduce income tax.'

The rumor that I was a sore loser to a poor investment decision continued as lawyers and judges went out of their way to make me responsible for loopification;

'In critical legal studies, the collapse of a legal distinction resulting when two ends of a continuum become so similar that they become indistinguishable. For example it may be impossible to distinguish "public" from "private"' because of loopification.'

The ABCP *'Crisis in Canada'* Report ascribed the same fakery to ABCP off-the bankbook unnumbered tied loans that do not count in a credit rating system. A gullible tax-credit saver has no idea of yield on debt hidden from the Treasury, not reported in the budget, which is the Magna Carta Loophole.

Bank *'ABCP Tax Arbitrage Ponzi Principal Collections'* delivered my Subprime Mortgage CDS tax-saver losses owed on paper to the ABCP *'Holder'* in a shadow bank and the same again to recapitalize tax-credit notes on paper due to taxpayer losses owed to an ABCP *'Holder'* in private retail bank and public central bank balances paid twice over— collect through court estoppel;

*'A judicial determination that a conversion has taken place — **though in truth one has not** — because a defendant has been estopped from offering a defense.'*

Software errors *'loopify'* unwanted results of computer code mostly checked-out before implementation. Worst cases, such as aircraft control software that overrides human-flight control can be disastrous until loops are fixed, but court estoppel is constructive conversion;

'Conversion consisting of an action that in law amounts to the appropriation of property.'

All the lawyering to confuse and deny trial for me to defend was all in aid of section 165(3) to estop;

'Estop is a verb meaning to impede by estoppel, which is a legal restraint that prevents one from contradicting one's own previous statement.'

Bank clients fell into the estop trap that once asked if a signature signed on a bank loan demand note albeit rubberstamped and filled out for an accredited personal amount of net-worth afforded to invest in a tax shelter deal after it was signed was their signature. If yes they were snared by estop they couldn't deny or amend their own testimony that they signed a promise to pay bank money lent of its own accord to invest.

Mine was different as the note was doubled to twice the cost of 1 unit and interest changed and initialed that when the ICAO questioned Perris, he said it was initialed by the bank, not by him, and not by me.

I admitted the signature was mine, but not initialed by me to change the bank rate of interest, which because I could prove I was not present the day it was dated, it must have been tricked, or forged, to double up one sale commingled with another in the one loan account sued to collect regardless. The bank was hoisted on its own petard that judges had to rule the 165(3) a-bank-is-never-wrong law to deny my day in court.

The estop contradiction that a sworn lie notarized by a Commissioner for Taking Affidavits which cannot be denied is mistook by regulatory arbitrage conversion;

'Conversion by taking a chattel out of the possession of another with intention of exercising a permanent or temporary dominion over it, despite the owner's entitlement to use it at all times.'

And, ABCP *'Acquire-to-Distribute'* wrongful disposition;

'Conversion by depriving an owner of goods by giving some other person a lawful title to them.'

I kept a what-next diary to write my bankbook story.

Bank lawyering was long enough to publish the scam called *'The Perfect Sting'* in 2006. I don't remember how it happened, but Hamilton CHTV invited me to be interviewed on 5:30 Live, which was a real pleasure.

The director invited the forensic accountant involved in the affair representing some 150 investors in debt to bank tied loans in the scam. I told my story what happened to me, and he explained the debt, advising people to find a good financial advisor they could trust.

I had saved tax credits into personal financial ruin and notional national debt, and the justice system ruled no evidence of any wrongdoing by fraudulent conversion;

'Conversion that is committed by the use of fraud, either in obtaining the property, or withholding it.'

The law had the bank effect of involuntary conversion;

'The loss or destruction of property through theft, causality, or condemnation.'

Theft, causality, or condemnation, had all been leveled at Perris who was found guilty, but all his clients were accountable to pay his bank effect of causation;

'Securities: The fact that that an investor would not have engaged in a given transaction if the other party had made truthful statements at the required time.'

Looking back, it is difficult for me to understand why the bank filed its CCAP system in court as it clearly structured regulatory arbitrage to foreseeable cause;

'A cause that a reasonably prudent person would not anticipate or be expected to avoid.'

The lawyer for my appeal for trial advised to write the Minister of Justice and Attorney General of Canada, Hon Rob Nicholson, to intervene in the Perris affair on behalf of Canadian taxpayers in collective interest.

I took his advice and carried on writing for years.

A Ponzi pyramid gives a quick impression of fraud that I featured it as a cover page of analysis in a letter to Sir John Vickers, Chair of the ICB, about the need for taxpayer protection that I copied to my usual list.

But there was no reply from Sir John, ICBS Chair, or Mr. Mervyn, Governor of the Bank of England, or Lord Turner, Chairman of the FSA, or Mr. Mark Carney, Governor of the Bank of Canada, or James Flaherty, Minister of Finance Canada, or Jack Layton, Leader of the NDP, or Andrea Horwath, MPP, Hamilton Center.

Technically, tax scams rob the Crown so I addressed my Private Information for Public Prosecution of novel criminal acts to Her Royal Highness Queen Elizabeth the Second to somehow atone for my gullibility.

I sent it to Prime Minister of Canada, Stephen Harper, Minister of Justice and Attorney General of Canada, Rob Nicholson, Minister of Finance, James Flaherty, the Premier of Ontario, Justices of the Peace, and Chiefs of Police, without effect, except the Minister of Justice wrote me about it being my personal problem;

Department of Justice   Ministère de la Justice
Canada   Canada

Ottawa, Canada
K1A 0H8

JUN 2 0 2012

Dear Mr. Crawford;

On behalf of the Honourable Rob Nicholson, Minister of Justice and Attorney General of Canada, I acknowledge receipt of your correspondence concerning your personal situation. I regret the delay in responding.

I understand why you have written to the Minister and asked for assistance. I sympathize with the difficulties that you have experienced and realize that this situation has been distressing for you. However, as Minister of Justice and Attorney General of Canada, Minister Nicholson is mandated to provide legal advice only to the federal government. I hope you understand that, for this reason, he is not able to provide legal advice to members of the public or become involved in matters of a private nature. Similarly, neither department officials nor members of his staff are in a position to help resolve personal legal issues.

The most useful suggestion that I can offer, given your situation, is to continue to seek the advice of a lawyer in private practice to determine the course of action that will best serve your needs.

Thank you for writing.

Yours sincerely,

Manager
Ministerial Correspondence Unit

I had reported a detailed account of tax deductible securities fraud just to be told it was my problem!

But no reply, still nothing confuted and nothing done.

Except, Sir Mervyn who still talked about wrongdoing;

"What I hope is that everyone, everyone, now understands that something went very wrong with the U.K. banking industry. And we need to put it right."

The approved solution was to *'ring-fence'* investment banking from commercial personal risk due to various tax scams and money laundering schemes with LIBOR fixed interest on highly favorable hedged bets.

English is more fanciful that *'ring fenced'* seemed to imply authority. That something might be done. It had the sense of what Gary Cohn of Goldman Sachs had said when the WSJ reported his remedy, in 2009;

'There should be segregation of the retail deposit base and capital-markets activity.'

Newspapers seemed to engage readers in conversation between ICB – Independent Commission on Banking, Sir John Vickers and Lord Turner reported to advise;

'...the commission should not be constrained by any assumption that the, "present complex structures of banks always deliver vital social benefits – too often indeed, they reflect the objectives of tax avoidance and regulatory arbitrage."'

I had learnt about securities fraud, tax avoidance and evasion, and rent seeking tax arbitrage, but regulatory arbitrage was new. It was something to think about.

After 9 years as Bank of England Governor since 2003, Sir Mervyn King retired defending his position as he rejected criticism on BBC Radio in May 2012;

'My main point was not to try to blame anyone— this was a failure of the system,' he stated in the news.

Sir Mervyn King weighed in with 3 R's on BBC News to reform banking, Regulation, Resolution, Restructure.

He endorsed the ICB – Independent Commission on Banking, chaired by Sir John Vickers to restructure the system. The main idea to *'ring-fence'* high-street bank financials in retail operations, in case of a credit event on the investment side of the business, he said,

"It is vital that Parliament legislates to enact these proposals sooner rather than later."

Blaming a system requires data analysis to review.

My work on system analysis progressed nicely. But, it was as fatal to discuss implications of bad banking outside the judicial system, as much as it was within.

I sent my Private Information for Public Prosecution to the Minister of Justice and Attorney General of Canada to intervene for Canadians to protect the economy. But I didn't know he had a conflict of interest as Defendant for the Crown in the COMER affair.

By the time Minister of Justice and Attorney General, Rob Nicholson refused to intervene on a public matter, which he defined my personal problem, the lawyering against me was done. Indeed, I quite expected to have nothing more to do than just to retire in peace.

It was a last effort that I took my testimony to the House of Commons in Canada, but MPs refused to meet me about how Perris tax scams worked. They all said there was no public interest in alleged private losses in millions and public losses in billions.

It was reviewed by several authorities that everyone thanked me for my work. No one denied the tort and no one disagreed with my conclusion to recommend a bank transaction code to solve a transparency problem for the sake of securing the tax supply in the Treasury.

I returned to England, where MP John Mann told me he had sent my Bank Whistleblower testimony to the Treasury Select Committee, still waiting reply.

It was different in England that newspapers reported Sir John and Sir Mervyn and Lord Turner in such a different light of concern to do something that I had never seen in Canada. There was more news about Mark Carney and his Bank of Canada résumé to the Bank of England to fix banking how new government said it should be. I wrote Mr. Andrew Tyrie, Chair of the Parliamentary Commission on Banking Standards in August 2012, and I went to London to a session at Grimond Room, Portcullis House, in November.

I passed security and was directed to the committee room to wait in the public area until debate was over.

After an interesting discussion they were wrapping up to leave when I stood up and introduced myself to offer my submission in person. There was a quick reaction by security that two officers flanked me and members of the public were told to leave. I discussed my writing the Chair and someone took my papers and guards saw me out the building, and that was the end of that.

ICBS sent a letter of thanks for my interest, but that was all, so I returned to Canada to continue writing.

~~~~~~~~~~~

18. Constitutional Class Action Lawsuit

When Minister of Justice and Attorney General, Rob Nicholson advised me find a lawyer in June 2012, I had no idea he was Defendant in the COMER Action, which I knew little about, until a year or two later.

As much as I was reeling from heavy handed lawyering I was willing to assist COMER as an expert witness.

It was ironic my work on bank system design, built to defraud taxpayers was chapter-and-verse for me to analyze a legal loophole in the socioeconomic system.

I listened and learned Ruly English as it was spoken by Rocco Galati for William Krehm and Ann Emmett claiming tort in breach of the Canadian Constitution;

'The fundamental and organic law of a nation or state, establishing the conception, character, and organization of its government, as a well as prescribing the extent of its sovereign power and the manner of its exercise.'

When Galati confirmed I would be called as an expert witness if ever it came to trial, I took it upon myself to refine my understanding of money rules of law in context of system analysis for binary code construction;

'The act of building by combining or arranging parts or element; the thing so built. Act or process of interpreting or explaining the sense or intention of a writing.'

Anyone writing computer code to process code of law has to separate the practical from intent, which is distinguished as literal or strict construction;

'An interpretation that considers only the literal words of a writing.'

Or, it is an equitable or liberal construction;

'An interpretation that applies to a writing in light of the situation presented and that tends to effectuate the spirit and purpose of the writing.'

My sense of construction focused on constitutionalism expressed in COMER arguments for and against trial as litigation continued through 2017. It allowed me to consider ambiguity-avoiding rules to construe proper Ruly English to test the logic of socioeconomic system gap analysis for any constitutional challenge;

'A lawsuit claiming that a law or government action is unconstitutional.'

COMER, a Toronto based economic *'Think Tank'* had filed a lawsuit in 2011 that on October 14, 2015 the Crown argued against trial and instead recommended an alternative approach to liberal constructionism. The Crown advised an Action against the Bank of Canada, as to the word *"may"* in section 18, should be tried in the real case of any town being refused a cheap loan.

Galati had filed an <u>AMENDED</u> STATEMENT OF CLAIM (Pursuant to s17(1) and (5)(b) Federal Courts Act, and s24(1) and 52 of the Constitution Act, 1982a *'Proposed Class Action Proceeding'* on March 26, 2015.

He positioned his reply in 3 counter arguments,

"One is— he does what the Court of Appeal says he shouldn't do: He doesn't take the facts as pleaded. He reconstitutes the claim in his hypothetical analysis."

"...The Crown cannot by its construction of the Respondent's claim make it say something which it does not say."

Justice Russell asked Galati to be more specific,

"Oh, for instance he goes on and on about treaty rights. Nobody is pleading treaty rights. He says he has no clue what the abdication of governments is here. It's very clear in the pleadings: The Minister of Finance has given to a group of private bankers in Basel, Switzerland the right to tell what the Bank of Canada should do. And the Minister of Finance under the Bank of Canada Act is a shareholder of the shares of the bank in trust for Her Majesty the Queen. It can't be clearer than that. It's in the pleadings, for example."

Justice Russell asked if it was the only example that Galati continued,

"I'd ask Your Lordship when you're reviewing my friend's submissions to ask yourself: Is this what the pleadings say or is it what Mr. Hajacek is saying?"

"Secondly, my friend goes on at length about the supremacy of Parliament. No dispute there. Every single case that he put before you on the supremacy of Parliament is missing one critical element with respect to the case before you: None of those cases involve the constitutional issue."

"Yes, Parliament can be — they can be as nincompoop as much as they want, as long as they don't inflict constitutional violations."

Justice Harris laughed in appreciation of a startling revelation in legal wit,

"Heehaw, that's very reassuring, thank you, tshew."

"I know, but that's the law," Galati continued dryly, *"However, that's <u>not</u> the case before you."*

Galati pressed the real reason for trial was the budget,

"The case before you is that there is an executive breach of a constitutional requirement by the Minister of Finance with respect to the budget process, and that as a result the legislation that comes out of Parliament breaches the constitutional right to no taxation without representation. Why? The MP's are blindfolded."

"Which is intrinsically tied and inseparable from the right to vote both under the Elections Act and section 3 of the Charter, which constitutionalizes the right to vote in the Federal elections Act."

He paused to clarify voting rights,

"The right to vote includes the right to effective representation. If the MPs are blindfolded by executive constitutional breaches by the Minister of Finance, how does that ensure effective representation?"

Galati explained the constitutional breach,

"So what comes out of Parliament comes out with the constitutional breach. My friend says, yeah, but you can't force him to legislate. There's no constitutional right to legislate. That's nonsense... The Supreme Court of Canada says omissions are subject to constitutional review for constitutional breaches."

Galati rejected the idea the claim was for legislation,

"Now, that's another instance where my friend says that I'm asking Parliament to legislate. I'm saying that nowhere in the pleadings are we asking Parliament to legislate. We are simply saying that there's an abdication of executive and parliamentary duty with respect to the budget pleaded. That is a different matter."

Galati explained failure to act in justiciability,

"And the failure to act applies equally to the executive as it does to the legislature with respect to constitutional breaches, and we get that pre-Charter and post-Charter from law."

"...when I get back to justiciability — I will now start in on my argument with respect to the facts that are in my factum at tab 8 of my motion record."

Galati explained justiciability from the previous ruling,

"With respect, and it's going to sound bizarre but this is the way it was played out, but with respect to the justiciability of declaratory relief that Your Lordship did not strike in April last year, you are yourself issue estopped. There's issue estoppel and res judicata that applies. What your judgment says... essentially you said that you ruled in your ruling that the declaratory relief that was sought was justiciable. However, the tort claims under section 7 and 15 of the Charter suffered and therefore you were striking the whole thing to re-amend. But it's clear from your decision that that is with respect to tort claims, and you left the jurisdiction standing hanging pending the amendment. That is what your judgment says."

Galati explained the Crown challenged the ruling,

"That is how my friend understood it... my friend took issue with your judgment, one, that you erred in fact and law in finding that that there were alleged breaches of issue in the Plaintiffs amended statement of claim that ere justiciable. Two, the judge erred in law by finding section 18 of the Bank of Canada Act could not be interpreted in a motion to strike but would require full legal argument on the full evidentiary record."

Justice Russell wanted to see the written claim,

"This is your statement of claim?"

"Yes."

"And it's at tab?"

Galati located the written submission,

"Seven, seven. Very briefly, at page 207 of the motion record — which is paragraph 1-A-8 of the statement of claim, we seek declaratory relief with respect to the taxation and voting issue. It's framed there is an inseparable breach tied to the right to vote. Then at paragraph 41 we plead the executive breach of the constitutional duty with respect to the budgetary process and how that inseparably links to the constitutional breach of no taxation without representation as it's tied to the right to vote under section 3, and as it's tied to the Bank of Canada, which is federal legislation."

And Galati explained the origins in the Magna Carta,

"My friend also misstates my argument in that he says that I ground this right in the Magna Carta. That's not the case. If you read the pleadings, I simply state that the right to no taxation without representation has its genesis in the Magna Carta, but it was articulated in the English Bill of Rights, codified in sections 53, 54, and 90 of our Constitution Act, and post-patriation... it's still part of our constitutional law."

Galati referred to the factum about the budget,

"My discussion of the budget issues is contained at pages 237 to 240 of my factum, and I won't read it all."

He explained the budget loophole,

"Moreover, what is missed is the primary duty which is constitutional in the budgetary process outlining all revenues and expenditures as historically evolved from the Magna Carta and tied to the constitutional right to no taxation without representation."

"At paragraph 22, I set out the codification of these principles in section 53, 54, and 90, and then state that by removing and not revealing the true revenues of Parliament, which is the only body which can constitutionally impose tax and thus approve the proposed spending from the speech from the throne, the Minister of Finance is removing the elected MPs' ability to properly review and debate the budget, and pass its expenditure and corresponding taxing provisions through the elected representatives of the House of Commons."

Galati dealt with the novel argument issue,

"Now, there isn't a lot of tax constitutional litigation that goes on, apart from the division of power context, even under the Charter. The fact that it's novel is neither here nor there... In fact, the fact that it's novel should be allowed to proceed so long as it's clearly not frivolous and vexatious. Leading justiciability even on the new declaratory relief sought, the new constitutional violation sought, it's not plain and obvious that this is a frivolous and vexatious case."

The lawyer referred to the four-point qualifying test,

"My friend says, where's the statute with the federal statutory underpinning, under the test?

And how it had been passed without fail,

"Well, you've got the Bank of Canada Act, which you found was an underpinning in your ruling on the declaratory ruling with respect to the Bank of Canada; and you've got the Elections Act, with the right to vote, which is codified under section 3 of the Charter; and you have a Minister of the Crown who's subject to a federal tribunal under section 2 of the Federal Court Act, and section 17 of the Federal Court Act which allows for actions for declaratory relief."

Galati set out the legal conundrum,

"So you have federal actors under federal legislation who are breaching constitutional norms and rights with the effect of extinguishing a constitutional right of no taxation without representation."

To conclude his novel argument before the Court,

"So I fail to see how the jurisdictional test is not met. We are not seeking bare declaration of the interpretation of a constitutional provision without federal statutory or executive underlying acts or action. Both the underlying acts are federal."

That considering real issues all was left... is standing,

"My friend says: Where are the real issues? The deficit is real. The taxes they pay are real. The Bank of Canada issues are real. And so past jurisdiction, we are really left with standing. When I go to declaratory relief from paragraphs 28 to 29 in my factum, my friend is confused with one serious thing and I pray that the Court is not. He seems to think that to get declaratory relief you need a cause of action tied to it. And the Supreme Court of Canada has shot that down..."

Galati spoke to the non-private issue,

"The fact that there is a corresponding private request for relief with respect to taxes we say my clients are unconstitutionally being straddled with is fine, but even it that tort was not there, the declaratory relief can be sought in and by itself... It's not the procedural avenue of judicial review by way of application as opposed to by way of action. Under section 17 this Court has ruled one can seek declaratory relief by way of action, and that is in my factum."

Galati referred the Court to the law,

"But I can refer Your Lordship to paragraph 31, where I actually extract the portions... 'The constitutionality of legislation has always been a justiciable issue. The right of the citizenry to constitutional behavior by Parliament can be vindicated by declaration that legislation is invalid or that a public act is ultra vires.'"

And he wanted nothing inaccurate in paragraph 134,

"That is exactly what my clients seek with respect to the actions of the Minister of Finance and the resulting constitutional breach of their right to vote — of their right not to be taxed without effective representation by their MP's, because they're blindfolded by the Minister of Finance and what he does not deliver, which is a constitutional requirement... we say."

Nor misstate the Supreme Court in paragraph 140,

"The Courts are the guardians of the Constitution and cannot be barred by mere statutes from issuing a declaration on a fundamental constitutional matter. The principles of legality, constitutionality and the rule of law demand no less."

And with respect to a corporate brought challenge,

"Furthermore, the remedy available under this analysis is of a limited nature. A declaration is a narrow remedy. It is available without cause of action, and courts make declarations whether or not any consequential relief is available."

Galati referred to trilogy on the standing case,

"The Courts are quite capable to control declaratory actions, both through discretion by taking a stay and by imposing costs, and as a matter of experience, to which I will return. Does not seem to have been spawned by any inordinate number of taxpayers' actions to challenge the legality of municipal expenditures. A more telling consideration from me but not on the other side of the issue is whether the question of constitutionality should be immunized from judicial review by denying standing to anyone to challenge the impugned statute. That in my view is the consequence of the judgment below in the present case. The substantive issue raised by the Plaintiffs' action is a justiciable one, and prima facie it would be strange and indeed alarming if there was no way in which a question of alleged excessive legislative power, a matter traditionally within the scope of the judicial process, could be made the subject of adjudication."

Galati referenced pages 8 and 9 of the decision,

"...the Court deals with this notion that in public interest standing there could be other people who are better suited to bring on the action. In this case, they were arguing that maybe the attorney generals of the provinces with respect to the federal act..."

Galati specified what the Supreme Court had ruled,

"Page 8, the Supreme Court States:"

"The question of constitutionality of legislation has in this country always been a justiciable question. Any attempt by Parliament or the legislature to fix conditions precedent as by way of requiring consent of some public office or authority to the determination of an issue of constitutionality of legislation cannot foreclose the Courts merely because conditions remain unsatisfied."

Galati continued how the Court had ruled,

"Short of a reference either to a provincial appellate court by the Lieutenant Governor-in-Council or to this court by the Governor General-in-Council, is there any other way in which the validity of the statute— can be determined in a judicial proceeding when the federal attorney general has declined to act?"

Galati positioned his arguments for legal standing,

"So we have here in this case I say that my clients, because of constitutional violations to their constitutional rights with respect to taxation and right to vote, have personal standing. And if they don't have personal standing as the Prothonotary found, they have public interest standing."

Justice Russell checked standing with a statement,

"In terms of their personal standing, they're really in no different position from any other Canadian citizen, right? The disadvantages which they say they have suffered and the losses they say they have suffered we all have suffered as taxpayers."

Which Galati agreed,

"Yes, like Thorsen."

And, Justice Russell responded,

"Right."

Then Galati described the Court decision,

"Like in Thorsen. It doesn't mean — the fact that every Canadian citizen may be treated the same way under the constitutional breach does not mean that no Canadian citizen has personal standing."

Justice Russell asked about that in terms of scope,

"My question would be that any Canadian citizen could have brought this action?"

Galati confirmed the past ruling,

"Yes. And I'm going to get to that in standing. That's right. That is what Thorsen says. That was the ruling in Thorsen. This is a rate payer case. Any Canadian citizen could bring this, and they did. And in Thorsen they got standing."

Galati referred to Supreme Court of Canada rulings,

"When we're looking at standing, I have extracted in my arguments before now that as early as 1951 the Supreme Court of Canada ruled that the Constitution of Canada does not belong to either Parliament or to the legislature; it belongs to the country, and that is where the citizens of the country will find protection of the rights to which they are entitled."

"After all, the Constitution is a document for the people, and one of most important goals of any system of dispute resolution is to serve well those who make use of it."

Galati described COMER as if a Comer committee,

"So my clients want a committee that has been engaged and interested in the issues put before the Court for decades, and the two biological Plaintiffs who form part of that committee have brought this challenge forward. And they have the constitutional right to bring this judicial review of unconstitutional executive action and legislative omission which results in a constitutional violation of the right to no taxation without representation from the right to vote."

Galati concluded his argument on standing,

"So if we are looking with an eye to standing and the Constitution belongs to the citizen, and that executive in Parliament cannot exceed constitutional parameters, and judicial review writ large either by way of application or by action is available to declare actions and legislation unconstitutional. And given that the Constitution is entrenched, any and all citizens have a constitutional right, the public interest standing where they seek a declaration as to the constitutional validity or vires of executive action or legislation. Now because the way the common law evolves, I don't see in any discussion on the standing cases that anyone has ever put their mind to this dimension and how this has evolve with respect to standing."

Galati looked at his notes about Crown submissions,

"My friend went on about the duty to legislate. We are not arguing the duty to legislate. We are arguing the constitutional violations of abdicating their duty to govern which results in constitutional violations. They are two different kettle of fish."

Galati referred the Defense said about the budget,

"We say that the executive constitutional duty rests on the Minister of Finance with respect to the budgetary process, and by putting 'blinders' on the MP's with respect to true revenue, you get a constitutional breach of the constitutional right to no taxation without representation."

"...Again I reiterate that all the cases that my friend put to you with respect to parliamentary privilege that Parliament is the master of its own house. I have no disagreement with those, absent constitutional violations and absent exceeding constitutional parameters. All those case my friend brought before you did not have constitutional argument in them or challenge."

"My friend says that the committee is not a citizen and does not have the right to vote, but the amendments set out the 13 members of the steering committee of COMER. There are two biological Plaintiffs. The fact that they're in public interest standing, I was not directly affected by the new citizenship act. However, I got a public interest standing. The Constitutional Law Centre is an Ontario corporation. It got standing to challenge the provisions."

"Again— and I go back to my friend positing common law doctrines that have nothing to do with this case and ignoring the constitutional dimensions that are the crux of this case. The last thing I would like to remind the Court is that with respect to these issues, they are intertwined, the no taxation without representation, the deficit, and the connection is the executive prism who is the Minister of Finance who holds shares of the Bank of Canada in trust for Her Majesty the Queen or people of Canada, and who at the same time is constitutionally charged with the budget process."

Galati reviewed his *"Proposed Class Action Proceeding"*;

Court File No: T-2010-11

"Proposed Class Action Proceeding"

FEDERAL COURT
COUR FÉDÉRALE
FILED / DÉPOSÉ
MAR 2 6 2015
C. MOKBEL
TORONTO, ON

FEDERAL COURT

MOTION

BETWEEN:

COMMITTEE FOR MONETARY AND ECONOMIC REFORM ("COMER"),
WILLIAM KREHM, AND ANN EMMETT

Plaintiffs,

- and -

HER MAJESTY THE QUEEN, THE MINISTER OF FINANCE,
THE MINISTER OF NATIONAL REVENUE, THE BANK OF CANADA,
THE ATTORNEY GENERAL OF CANADA

Defendants,

AMENDED STATEMENT OF CLAIM
(Pursuant to s.17(1) and (5)(b) *Federal Courts Act*,
and s.24(1) and 52 of the *Constitution Act, 1982*)

TO THE DEFENDANT:

A LEGAL PROCEEDING HAS BEEN COMMENCED AGAINST YOU by the Applicant. The claim against you has been set out in the following pages.

IF YOU WISH TO DEFEND THIS PROCEEDING, you or your solicitor acting for you are required to prepare a statement of defence in Form 171B prescribed in the Federal Courts Rules, serve it on the applicant's solicitor, or where the applicant does not have a solicitor, serve it on the applicant, and file it, with proof of service, at the local office of this Court, WITHIN 30 DAYS after this statement of claim is served on you, if you are served within Canada..

Copies of the Federal Courts Rules, information concerning the local offices of the Court and other necessary information may be obtained on request to the Administration of the Court at Ottawa (telephone 613-992-4238) or at any local office.

IF YOU FAIL TO DEFEND THIS PROCEEDING, judgment may be given against you in your absence and without further notice to you.

Date: MAR 26 2015   Issued By;

"It's my respectful submission, My Lord, that really the flowing from your decision which was concerned with the insufficient pleadings with respect to the tort claims, which saw re-amendment, and your decision was endorsed by the Federal Court of Appeal, that the amendments that were made were very narrow and short with respect to the declaratory relief and constitutional violations and request for damages in terms of returning the portion of the tax paid on the deficit for the last 4 years by the Plaintiffs, personal Plaintiffs, and the fact that the justiciability and other issues with respect to the declaratory relief not struck that in the main this motion I would say with respect to my friend is a frivolous and vexatious motion. He is trying to unearth matters of res judicata. [9] *This motion was unwarranted in the sense that 80 per cent of it is res judicata, and the other 20 per cent is self-evident with respect to jurisdiction and standing."*

"Subject to any questions you may have, those are my submissions."

It is quite unlikely Comer Claimants understood what Galati was talking about; especially not aware they were named as representative Claimants in a Canada-wide Proposed Class Action. The Crown was quiet, and Justice Russell finished out the legal procedure,

"There's no reply? Okay. That being the case, I have a very interesting case to consider. I will go away and I will do that and get something out as soon as I can."

~~~~~~~~~~~

---

[9] Ref: Black's Law. An issue that has definitely been settled by judicial decision.

19. Comer Motions to Consider in Appeal

I take reasonably good notes at a conversational pace. But, the hearing for COMER was an important matter for me as a potential witness, so I requested the audio and transcript record of the proceedings.

For me the most significant outcome was advice from Justice Russell to Canadians that they should take up any complaint about the COMER struggle for trial with their Members of Parliament, which I did.

I wrote Oakville Riding MP John Oliver for a meeting to explain my study of *'Rent Seeking Tax Arbitrage'* and to request a Private Members Bill to debate apparent tort in a loophole. I went to his office and we discussed the bank effect of twice paid tax credit Windbills, which he promised to, follow up, but never got back to me.

It was the same old runaround, my representative did nothing, and he refused to meet me about COMER, as Prime Minister, Justin Trudeau, reportedly said;

'I don't believe in conspiracy theories.'

My professional interest in tort before the court was to follow tax revenue and to explain the banking system in context of alleged trillion dollar losses not reported to the Treasury hidden from the budget. Lawyers and judges had ruled on private commercial bank debt without trial, and now the Crown argued against trial of trillions of interest charged on billions of public debt without trial alleged the case in the COMER Action.

I reread my notes and listened to the Crown argue for its motion to strike. The idea that people could remedy Magna Carta Loophole Gullible Taxpayer Law telling MPs to change the law was hardly plausible.

Galati argued a good case for COMER, but there was a conflict: Justice Russell already decided justiciability for COMER and he was therefore estopped from ruling different than his decision by res judicata;

'An issue that has been definitely settled by judicial decision.'

Nevertheless, Justice Russell ruled against Canadian taxpayers for the Action in a lengthy decision with an Order for the Crown on February 8, 2016, on page 64;

ORDER

THIS COURT ORDERS that

1. The Plaintiffs' latest Amended Claim is struck in its entirety;
2. Leave to amend is refused;
3. Costs are awarded to the Defendants

The Justice Russell ruling did not go down well among Comer committee members that Justice Noël had to Order filed Motions removed, over Christmas 2016.

I was concerned my expert witness testimony would not be considered. So, I filed my academic work for peer review that a universal bank transaction control number would augment transparency in the banking system, especially with respect to a proper account of credit/debit balances through the budget process.

Comer committee claimant, Erick Bittschwam filed a motion for the Court to appoint an auditor to assess the financial impact of proven criminal LIBOR cost of bank loan-issued money, and government approved tax credits not reported in the budget hidden from the Treasury, to re-consider the COMER case for trial;

> FEDERAL COURT OF APPEAL.　　　DECEMBER 16, 2016
> MOTION
>
> BETWEEN:
>
> COMMITTEE FOR MONETARY AND ECONOMIC REFORM ("COMER"),
> WILLIAM KREHM, AND ANN EMMETT
>
> Plaintiffs,
>
> -and -
>
> HER MAJESTY THE QUEEN, THE MINISTER OF FINANCE,
> THE MINISTER OF NATIONAL REVENUE, THE BANK OF CANADA,
> THE ATTORNEY GENERAL OF CANADA
>
> Defendants,
>
> MOTION RECORD: Motion to Reconsider Pursuant to Rule 397(1).
>
> OVERVIEW: The appeal is about citizens' right to enjoy constitutional behaviors without need for causal Actions, in this case for a clarification of Bills of law that govern monetary issues and economic policy in Canada, that especially a declaratory judgment is required as a preventative measure in case of criminal acts that outdated laws from eleventh century judicial systems are plainly not applicable or enforceable in business affairs of the twenty first century.
>
> SPECIFICALLY: This Motion is to Reconsider the verdict to ensure Court awareness of real parties behind the Action being individual taxpayers and the Motion for Assessment is to understand the sovereign debt position after comparing Public Bank of Canada onshore cost of money to actual offshore cost of [criminal] LIBOR to print Canadian onshore legal tender, and interest and principal costs of Tax Credit payments offset to government distributions of public wealth into private enterprise over the period specified in the original [COMER] Claim.

On June 20, 2016, the Registrar filed a letter from a lawyer that Erick Bittschwam was a <u>former</u> member of the Comer Steering Committee therefore was without standing. In addition, COMER Plaintiffs as Appellants, disassociated themselves and opposed the motion and strenuously stated the motion not be accepted as filed, and if accepted, it should be purged from the Court Record Pursuant to Federal Court Rule Number 74.

The Order was executed through the justice system.

Court DIRECTION to purge the Motion to Reconsider and Appointing an Assessor was dated July 25, 2016, and Bittschwam was warned off the case.

Steering Committee members for COMER who read the court record: Galati described Members of Parliament as nincompoops, the Crown characterized lawmakers as fickle *'Will o' Wisp'* thinkers. He said the budget was rigged to secret tax redistributions from fiscal account.

But, as much as Crown prayers for a Motion to Strike a COMER Amended Statement of Claim and pleadings for trial were lessons about the Constitution of Canada, there was no real estimate of tax-revenue loss.

The bank system hid the true account from the public.

Erick described his requirement of the Court in terms of his right to enjoy constitutional behaviors without need for causal Action; in this case for clarification of law that governs monetary issues and economic policy in Canada, that especially a declaratory judgment is required as a preventative measure in case of criminal acts. And outdated laws from eleventh century judicial systems are probably not applicable, or should not be enforced, in the twenty first century.

His Motion to Reconsider was pursuant to Rule 397(1) and for Appointing an Assessor pursuant to Rule 52 to ensure Court awareness of the real parties behind the COMER Action being individual taxpayers wanting to measure and understand the sovereign debt position comparing Public Bank of Canada onshore cost of money to offshore cost of LIBOR to print Canadian onshore legal tender, and interest and principal costs of tax credits offset to government redistributions of public wealth into private enterprise over the period specified in the Amended Statement of Claim.

Another letter JAN 3, 2017 described the so-called *'Misguided'* Motion to Reconsider and for Appointing an Assessor not relevant to the COMER Appeal. So, it was removed pursuant to Rule 74 on JAN 25, 2017;

CONTAINS DOCS No. 21-23
CONTENT LES DOCS No.

Court File No: A-76-16

FEDERAL COURT OF APPEAL

BETWEEN:

COMMITTEE FOR MONETARY AND ECONOMIC REFORM ("COMER"), WILLIAM KREHM, AND ANN EMMETT

Plaintiffs/Appellants

- and -

HER MAJESTY THE QUEEN, THE MINISTER OF FINANCE, THE MINISTER OF NATIONAL REVENUE, THE BANK OF CANADA, THE ATTORNEY GENERAL OF CANADA

Defendants/Respondents

MOTION RECORD

(Motion in Writing Pursuant to Rule 369 re Federal Appeal Court File A-76-16 Judgment *"Appeal is dismissed with costs"* for a Motion to Reconsider Pursuant to Rule 397 (1)(a), and a Motion for Appointing an Assessor Pursuant to Rule 52 (1)(a) and (b)

In accordance with the Direction of The Honourable Chief Justice Noël dated January 24, 2017, this document has been removed from the Court file pursuant to Rule 74.
JAN 25 2017

Claimant/Plaintiff/Appellant
Erick Bittschwam
Named Claimant in File T-2010-11

The Comer Claimant complained he was denied rights,

"I am Erick Bittschwam, I have been named in perhaps the most important lawsuit in Canadian banking history. Constitutional attorney, Rocco Galati, has been defending Canadian taxpayers' legal interests regarding the cost of money and lack of budgetary transparency which conceals distribution of public wealth to private entities."

"On December 7, 2016, the Federal Court of Appeals ruled against the trial of the case against the Bank of Canada, striking in its entirety with costs awarded to the defendants. Thinking that there may have been an error due to procedural omission I served a motion to reconsider to the court on December 16, 2016."

"During a Federal Court of Appeal hearing on October 14, 2015 brought against the Bank of Canada in May of 2008 by William Krehm and Rocco Galati, it was said that, '...the wisdom of legislation is not an area of interest to the courts. If Parliament, which is singularly powerful in matters of taxation does not receive adequate information to make meaningful decisions, the only remedy is for people who also do not have adequate information... is to exercise your constitutional democratic power, at least every five years, and vote in a party that would pass a different law.'"

"I'm urging the citizenry of Canada to do more than exercise their democratic rights, every now and again, and take an active interest in the doings of their bank, the Bank of Canada. And, assure that they have an adequate understanding of its workings that monetary and fiscal policy is – what it is – and that the wisdom of legislation be known."

"Apparently, this court case file number A76-16 is closed, with no recourse as of December 7th 2016."

"My motions for an assessor and reconsideration were viewed with what feels like extreme prejudice. And a motion record of respondents was sent to me on January 10th 2017. My first reaction to this brief were having received a thinly veiled unspecified threat clearly describing my positioning as being irrelevant and vexatious and of me being as it were, an off-the street outsider."

Bittschwam spoke as did Emmett, and he wanted to stand on side, but Justice Gleason ruled him without standing, and wrote my work not relevant. Krehm was incorporated so the only representative taxpayer in the COMER affair was just Ann Emmett, and no one else;

Federal Court of Appeal   **Cour d'appel fédérale**

TO : Appeal Registry
FROM : Gleason J.A.
DATE : July 25, 2016
RE : A-76-16
Committee for Monetary and Economic Reform et al. v. Her Majesty the Queen et al.

DIRECTION

The Motion Records received, but not filed, from the proposed parties (Anthony Crawford and Erick Bittschwam) shall be returned to them as neither has sought or been granted standing in this appeal and the issues raised in the proposed parties' Motion Records are irrelevant to this appeal.

"Mary J.L. Gleason"
J.A.

"I'm somewhat confused as I distinctly remember reading my name as one of COMER's steering committee members in prior court filings. At the very least, I am a Canadian citizen that has requested a legitimate audit, in effect seeking some clarity as to the workings of our bank, which apparently is not acceptable, irrelevant, and vexatious if attempted through court procedure."

Then he asked for what only a judge could do,

"What then do you suppose, is a legitimate respectable means?"

As well as Comer Committee Chair, Ann Emmett was the key spokesperson that she and Galati continued to promote COMER to whoever would listen, and maybe join the cause to change the law— to reform banking.

When the Canadian Alliance of Seniors recognized her work, Emmett expressed her heartfelt thanks, and she reminded the audience of her raison d'être, saying,

"Show whether the law works or not! We have to show the difference between what is legal and what is just, when what is legal is not synonymous with what is just. And, when the law doesn't work,"

Emmett turned her gaze to look Galati in the eye,

"...then we have to politically change the law."

Galati nodded in agreement as the audience endorsed Emmett, who was loudly praised in lengthy applause.

~~~~~~~~~~~

20. COMER 2017 Ruling in Review

Once the courts removed offending motions purged in January, the Supreme Court of Canada continued to proceed with the Application of Appeal for trial for COMER in February 2017. It was dismissed in a brief Coram ruling of 9 judges on May 4, 2017.

Rocco Galati for COMER held a meeting for the press at his office with William Krehm and Ann Emmett and other committee members to discuss the decision.

William Krehm was 93 when he sued the government of Canada to comply with the law in 2008.

He was 98 when he sued for justice in 2011 and 102 when he outlived 6 years lawyering through 2015. He had stood before the Federal Court bench during his hearing for trial denied in 2012. He was in a wheelchair through proceedings in 2015 and later when Justice Russell denied trial in 2016. He was 103 when he was denied his day in court, which he took to the Court of Appeal in 2016. And, the Supreme Court of Canada ruled against Appeal in 2017, and he died at the age of 105 in 2019.

There was another meeting for COMER members after the press release that was recorded for people to see on the COMER Webpage. Krehm, Emmett and Galati left his office to plan what next in June 2017.

The meeting was organized for COMER members only. It excluded a few from the Comer Committee, I was a member and I took a picture of Erick Bittschwam as he greeted his old friend William Krehm. It was the last time I attended a COMER meeting. It was special with quite a number of supporters in attendance as they had always been for William Krehm and his lawsuit.

A new chairperson, Herb Wiseman started the meeting and passed out a handout of the COMER press release for people to read and to ask questions.

Questions started with a reflective angle, *'What if?'*

"Could you speculate on what would have been the outcome had the Supreme Court given us this Appeal? What would the rest of the case look like after that?"

Galati ventured into legal speculation,

"I think the Supreme Court recognized the magnitude of the issue just like Justice Russell, the reason he reversed himself from the first to the second motion to strike, er, denied the, er, because this is the first time this issue is coming to them. And, it's probably blind deference to the political process that the court was too afraid to test this. Because, it really is, it's seismic in terms of the implications and the issues."

Galati described the outcome as it might have been,

"...So, if they had allowed it to proceed, you know the government would have had to put up, or shut up."

He reviewed legal alternatives,

"They'd have to defend. The facts were difficult to contest. And so, one of two things would have happened, either we'd get the constitutional declaration, or, I don't know, maybe it might have pushed the government to run the Bank of Canada, I don't know. So that's, that's what I think would have happened, one of the two."

Galati referred back into to the recent history of the case, and the financial impact of a government with a reputation of being above the law;

"...I don't think we'd have lost the case if it was allowed to proceed, because there's nothing in the case that was difficult to prove historically, or in terms of impact. There was nothing in the case that was difficult to prove in terms of their ignoring the legislation, and there was really nothing they could say in response."

"To be honest with you, in private conversations with council on the other side, he and I would argue these things together at the Department of Justice nearly 32 years ago. Yeah, he told me, this case is causing me lack of sleep. It's er, the issues are serious and to have to get to the merits; it was going to be hard."

The next question was more about tactics,

"And, if we had started the case what would the case then look like unfolding in terms of number of years. What kind of things we'd have to do?"

Galati considered strategy how to proceed if the case had been allowed leave, and how quick it might be,

"Well, I think we could have done this..." he paused,

"A lot of the facts would have been, I think a lot of the facts... we could have gone on a brief statement of facts in terms of historical chronology. And, then we just would have probably gone... we could have gone by Summary Judgment in terms of affidavit evidence on the economic theory and the economics of it. We could have done the first level of it in under a year and gone back to the Supreme Court in two and half years, easy."

Galati confirmed his estimation, *"Yea, easy,"*

And then he explained the Press Release, which was already on the COMER Webpage to see the video.

"What we've tried to make clear in the press release is that the Supreme Court of Canada never issues reasons when they deny leave. And, the reason for this is, they don't want to tell, they don't want anybody to know the reasons. There is actually jurisprudence Case Law from the Supreme Court where they say clearly and unequivocally that their refusing permission to hear a case is not to be misread that they are endorsing the correctness of the case down below. It's simply they don't want to hear the case at that particular time."

Galati suggested a few reasons he was denied trial,

"They could deny me on an issue two or three times… The reasons for denying me were very complex and multiple. On this one if I had to take an educated guess, it's the enormity of the issues, and a sense that we could pull a Pontius Pilot on this, wash our hands of it, not that there's no constitutional arguments, to address, but we'll leave it to the political process. That's a very likely sort of thing… that's going through their mind."

Galati was reflective as he spoke of social engineering,

"And also they didn't feel comfortable dealing with socio economic issues. Before the Charter came in the Supreme Court dealt with all sorts of socioeconomic issues… passed judgment on Pierre Trudeau's wage and price controls, if you remember those…"

But, there was also the globalization factor,

"The courts, because they're also too being angled by the corporate globalized agenda. They, they're almost, you know, hesitant to deal with these types of issues. Er, but so it's not that they technically agree, or disagree with the lower court, it's simply they didn't want to hear it."

Except, the chance of being granted leave,

"And, only eight or ten percent of the cases ever get permission, so er, you know, we will not know why these Supreme Court judges didn't grant leave, it's easy to speculate— but it doesn't mean they agree with the case down below."

The next discussion was a question of democracy,

"How do we know that justice is being done the law is being followed, if they're not excluding themselves, under they have arbitrary power?"

"They do have arbitrary power."

"Okay."

"As lawyers we never say the Supreme Court is right, they're just last. They don't make the right decision; they just make the last decision."

"So, where's the democracy, openness, transparency?"
"It's lacking. It's lacking, that's..." He thought about it, and said, *"...that's the imperfection of the system."*

Someone asked if the Appeal had changed the law,

"Does the disallowance of the appeal produce any law?"

Galati was quick to dispel any hope of justice,

"No! You can't mistake a refusal of leave as anything but, refusal of leave. So, it doesn't produce any law... The Federal Court of Appeal decision that what it says, you know, 'I'm upholding Justice Russell striking this because on the facts of the case you can't seek this declaratory relief'."

Galati spoke of courtrooms as playrooms for judges,

"The game they play is... on similar facts another judge may say, 'Okay, I'm going to hear the merits now'."

"Okay, so it doesn't produce any sort of roadblock?"

"No, no. That's not to say I suggest you start over again tomorrow... you need a novel factual context."

Galati continued to suggest a novel argument,

"Well, on this very issue, I think if you could convince a municipality to request, a provincial government to request loan, interest free loan, for human capital or infrastructure expenses, and the provincial government said no, that would be a very concrete, er, factual underpinning to take a run at it. But... I'm not here to encourage litigation; I'm just saying yes, there could be more than one matrix that would give rise to the same or similar issues with the same impetus and interest in the Bank of Canada and its interest free provisions."

Someone thought about doing it,

"Do you think a provincial government would be a slam dunk? Wouldn't it?"

"Yea, yea, if the provincial government just requested money..."

Chairman Wiseman was keen on the test idea,

"Rocco has just given us a very interesting strategy, which I think we should put on the table for further discussion... When we go to the municipality, it should be with a motion for them to apply for funding as opposed to just passing a motion saying it's a good idea."

Galati reconfirmed the legal approach in theory,

"They should request the Province to request 'X' amount of dollars for this 'Project' for this 'Program', through the Bank of Canada."

Wiseman still speaking for COMER seemed inspired,

"We've had a lot of motions and resolutions at the municipal level, but we've never had anyone go to that next step, which is to apply, and do a letter, get turned down, and take the legal route, which is an interesting option, and I'd never thought of it until now, and I thank you, Rocco, for that idea."

As I recall, Wiseman wasn't at the COMER hearing on October 14, 2015. He hadn't read the transcript how the Crown suggested taxpayers test the right to borrow cheap money from the Bank of Canada, as he'd have known it already, and he may have said as much.

The legacy of the COMER affair was greater awareness of the Canadian Constitution and role of the judiciary in government fiscal Ways and Means.

Taxpayers may not have known what really happened behind the scenes, except for this *'Truth of the Court'* and photographic record from the Federal Court.

It was my last time at a COMER meeting. There was no need for Comer members to continue to guide a Class Action for all taxpayers to sue for cheaper money and a transparent budget. Judges had ruled to strike down alleged tort without trial. It was over…

Sadly, I never saw William Krehm again. He died in April 2019 at the great age of 105.

~~~~~~~~~~~

Clockwise: 103 year old William Krehm reflects on his Supreme Court denied day in court in 2017. Crawford campaigns for NDP Identity Theft Protection in 2007. Crawford discusses Identity Theft card game with NDP Leader Howard Hampton in 2007. Crawford delivers NDP Petition 44 to Queen's Park in 2008 to reopen the OSC investigation of the Perris affair. London Occupy *'What would Jesus do?'* bank monopoly on the steps of St Paul's Cathedral in 2011. Crawford discussed INET *'Human After All'* Conference with Lord Adair Turner in 2014, and *'Great Divide'* with author Joseph Stiglitz, at Zurich University, FINEXUS Conference in 2018.

21. Will the Last Person Standing Please Sit Down

I had wanted to meet William Krehm after the Appeal to discuss his feelings about the outcome to mention in this book. It didn't happen, but I hope he heard me talk of COMER on CBC Radio on September 16, 2018.

CBC Cross Country Checkup is a weekend call-in for public opinion on all kinds of issues. My last call was to Rex Murphy about money a long time ago. This time it was about the political use of *'Notwithstanding'* law.

The call-in was about Ontario Premiere, Doug Ford, and his execution of law that questioned democratic ways in Canadian society,

"Our question today... who should have the final say on human rights in Canada, a judge, or politician? You are listening to Cross Country Checkup on CBC Radio."

Duncan McCue discussed the law with Tom Axworthy, Distinguished Fellow of Monk School of Global Affairs and Public Policy. He described the lawmaking system and the role of the judiciary,

"Politicians and legislators, they write the laws in the first place and you certainly want them to be cognizant of the Charter protection before they write the laws. Judges and the judiciary have a right and a tremendous contribution to interpret those laws, and the fact that they're independent and not elected gives them strength that the elected politicians do not have. Each has the role, they're equally valid in convention, how you approach rights, which shouldn't be in haste... So for the Premiere to say, 'I'm the only one who has a role, I have the democratic legitimacy,' is a basic misunderstanding of our constitution. There is a rule of law in the country protected by the independent judiciary."

Duncan McCue wanted a more in-depth history,

"So the rule of law, includes a 'notwithstanding' clause, it includes the option for a politician to take the step that they have taken. So I guess, as someone who was there at the table involved in the negotiations and saw the compromises that Prime Minister Trudeau had to make, or felt he had to make, to include the notwithstanding clause, here's my question for you: Does Canada still need a 'notwithstanding' clause?"

Tom Axworthy had been a player in Trudeau politics,

"I was not in favor of including section 33, and I would be much more relieved if we didn't have that temptation of allowing legislators and politicians like Doug Ford to take rights away and use a majority democracy. One can argue that was a necessary compromise to get the idea of the Charter accepted at a time when the idea of a Charter itself was contentious. So one can defend that makeup of that decision, but at the time, and in Cabinet, many argued that this was a danger, and that we were having a poisoned Charter by allowing the opt-out for politicians and so it is proven a generation later."

"That was Tom Axworthy, an advisor to former Prime Minister, Pierre Trudeau... You're listening to Cross Country Checkup on CBC Radio One, call us at..."

CBC continued conversation with constitutional expert Professor Allan Hutchinson of York University Osgoode Hall Law School. He advised, that in his opinion, the notwithstanding law was used wisely for the most part. He said it could probably not be overturned as it would open up too much controversy in contentious review.

One caller was concerned about tyrannical politics, which the professor expected in democratic society,

"I think one of the great challenges in any democracy; we look beyond Canada, or certainly within Canada, but also broadly, to say that the great challenge for democracy is that it simply doesn't mean that the majority gets to do whatever they want. We say the majority rules, but there are limits and restrictions on what they can do. And finding that balance and deciding what forum decides where that balance is, goes to the very heart of democracy."

Duncan McCue probed for a current example in law,

"Let's make this less abstract, how does the judiciaries' role in interpreting the Charter, which eventually led to the legalization of same sex marriage, how did that work, vis-à-vis the relation with Parliament?

"I think... one has to remember this was a large issue, it was a very important issue, there was a lot of public support for the move, and also one has to ask, I mean politicians... one of the great advantages of the Charter for politicians is they can pass-off controversial issues, and say, 'Hey, we didn't decide that, it was the Courts. So, the courts do get used by democratically elected politicians. But I think that same sex marriage was a way that worked out."

The professor reviewed it in terms of democracy,

"Parliament had its say, the government had its say in court, they could have had an opportunity to say we'll utilize the notwithstanding clause. There was pressure on the government to do so, but it was resisted. I see democracy working well there, in that circumstance."

"Tony Crawford is on the line. Hi Tony, welcome to Checkup. When do you think, Tony, it's appropriate to use the notwithstanding clause in this country?"

"I think it was appropriate in this instance with Doug Ford, and I have a question for Professor Hutchinson."

"Okay."

"Yes, I'm referring to decision that came down against Doug Ford. It refers point number two, 'I will forgo detail analysis of every legal issue raised in this proceeding because of timely decision. So, my question is, how is it that one judge can come up with one decision, when the exact same decision, or exact same issue before another judge, and they go the other way? And, if you want specific Case Law I can refer you to it."

Professor Hutchinson confirmed that it happens,

"No, no, no, that happens all the time. Of course judges, I don't think pass themselves off, as being infallible, particularly in these difficult areas. If you think the constitution is in black and white, people would be mistaken. It's very much a grey area, because it has to evolve with the society. But, that's what the Appeal Process is for... this will go to the Provincial Court of Appeal, and ultimately could go to the Supreme Court of Canada, so it works itself out through the system. I think just when Belobaba had 4 or 5 days to decide this; I think he did a reasonable job. I don't think there's any reason to challenge his good faith. He did what he thought was appropriate under the constitution... to pass law."

Duncan McCue remarked on hasty law that Doug Ford had objected, and chose to rule, despite it,

"There have been some legal commentators who have suggested that Justice Belobaba twisted himself into a pretzel, to try to find a Charter reason to overturn this law?"

The Professor defended how Justice Belobaba ruled,

"I'm not sure about that... I think it is a mistake to think that judges don't have political leanings, inclinations, tendencies. Belobaba would have a view. But he was presented with arguments before the Court and he worked with those arguments, and gave an honest and good faith response. People can of course disagree. But simply to dispense with his judgment saying, 'he was appointed, I was elected, let's move on' it seems to me to miss the whole point that we don't live in a democracy, we live in a constitutional democracy, and there are ways to change that constitution and so we need to operate with that in mind."

I offered, *"Can I refer to the case that is the opposite?"*

"Sure."

"Well, I'm referring to a case that took simply years to go through the courts. And, it was a claim by, er, it's COMER, the Committee on Monetary and Economic Reform, and the main claimant was a hundred and four years old. And, the courts just strung this out, for year after year, after year, just hoping he would die. And eventually, when it came to the decision, Justice Russell, explained it to the people that they would have to complain to politicians if they didn't like the way the law had played out. And so, people are doing that. I've certainly done it. And then the other thing is about this case that it did go through the appeal process, and then it went to the Supreme Court of Canada, and Rocco Galati, constitutional lawyer for COMER was absolutely appalled. He put out a press release that said that the Supreme Court of Canada made no reasons whatsoever to simply throw it out."

Professor Hutchinson countered on free speech,

"Well, I can't speak to the details of that, but it seems to me that in a sense is a democracy."

Professor Hutchinson defined the limits of my rights,

"You are very critical of a court decision, that's fine and appropriate... The Charter protects your right to do that. I'm critical of decisions, but we can't expect the system to deliver judgments that we all agree in."

William Krehm and Ann Emmett may not have been so confident in judicial and political checks and balances as Professor Hutchinson on Cross Country Checkup.

Canadians would be fine with judgments if they came out of trial, but arbitrary rule against trial is a different matter of justice denied.

My want of justice failed that judges ruled evidence of bank loan dependent tax-deductible securities fraud not credible for trial in 2009;

COURT OF APPEAL FOR ONTARIO   DOCKET: C49171

Gillese, MacFarland and LaForme JJ.A.

Heard: January 30, 2009

On appeal from the order of Justice Harris of the Superior Court of Justice, dated June 27, 2008

APPEAL BOOK ENDORSEMENT

We see no error in the decision below. The essence of the defense in this matter is that the appellant failed to read the loan documentation when he took out the loan or at any point in the following ten-year period when he made payments on the loan. The loan documentation makes it clear there is no genuine issue for trial in relation to the Bank...

My study of the Magna Carta Loophole, which was my sworn testimony as a bank whistleblower, was ruled not relevant to banking for trial in 2016.

Galati planned one corporate, William Krehm, and one biological person, Ann Emmett to sue for nothing more than clarification of law. It meant Ann Emmett was the one and only real person in Canada standing to sue the government-banking-judicial triune system of law; which the Crown defended against trial, endorsed by retiring Chief Justice McLachlin in May 2017;

'...The request for an oral hearing is dismissed. The application for leave to appeal from the judgment of the Federal Court of Appeal, Number A-76-16, 2016 FCA 312, dated December 7, 2016, is dismissed with costs.'

	No. 37431
May 4, 2017	Le 4 mai 2017
Coram: McLachlin C.J. and Abella, Moldaver, Karakatsanis, Wagner, Gascon, Côté, Brown and Rowe JJ.	Coram : La juge en chef McLachlin et les juges Abella, Moldaver, Karakatsanis, Wagner, Gascon, Côté, Brown et Rowe
BETWEEN:	**ENTRE :**
Committee for Monetary and Economic Reform ("COMER"), William Krehm and Ann Emmett	Committee for Monetary and Economic Reform (« COMER »), William Krehm et Ann Emmett
Applicants	Demandeurs
- and -	- et -
Her Majesty the Queen, Minister of Finance, Minister of National Revenue, Bank of Canada and Attorney General of Canada	Sa Majesté la Reine, ministre des Finances, ministre du Revenu national, Banque du Canada et Procureur général du Canada
Respondents	Intimés
JUDGMENT	JUGEMENT
The request for an oral hearing is dismissed. The application for leave to appeal from the judgment of the Federal Court of Appeal, Number A-76-16, 2016 FCA 312, dated December 7, 2016, is dismissed with costs.	La demande pour la tenue d'une audience est rejetée. La demande d'autorisation d'appel de l'arrêt de la Cour d'appel fédérale, numéro A-76-16, 2016 FCA 312, daté du 7 décembre 2016, est rejetée avec dépens.
J.S.C.C.	

Courts have a way of ruling costs in judgments. Costs in my legal quagmire ran into tens of thousands of dollars. Any cost for any proceeding was always an award to the bank, or else no cost against either party. When my appeal for trial was denied the lawyer for the bank claimed $30,000 that because he was insistent for immediate payment, I paid it in cash, in his office.

The bills were counted, accepted and receipted before an independent witness, but later, the lawyer for the bank objected payment wasn't allowed in cash, and he lied was shortchanged a thousand dollars. I paid up the difference by cheque to the bank just to be rid of all the anger. It made no difference; he still carried on lawyering for bank releases for 2 more years.

COMER costs were not disclosed, only that Galati was frugal, which was appreciated and mentioned that the case for trial would never have been heard otherwise.

Following Justice Gleason writing Erick Bittschwam he had no standing and my testimony was not relevant, the COMER was dismissed. I did what Judge Russell told taxpayers to do, which was to complain to MPs.

My way of doing that was to meet my MP John Oliver in Oakville to discuss Double Presentment Twice Paid Tax Credit Windbill Cash Flow Deficit Dollars. But he didn't want to talk about it, any more than he wanted public debate of my private losses before the Court of Appeal Ontario, or my public losses in my tax shelter account before the Supreme Court of Canada.

The bank sued its trick loan 12 years before it was done. The bank got its money with signed releases as a judge deemed me and my wife signed consent to annul all counterclaims and cross-claims in the matter.

~~~~~~~~~~~

22. Private and Public Regrets

My private regret of deciphering law in constant stress of a 12 year lawsuit was that a TIA put an end to a career in academia that might have been.

A 12 year assault of legal-shock treatment constrained me to soliloquize rather than rationalize any academic thinking that a professorship was a lost opportunity.

However, I did learn money rules of law and Canadian history to follow court advice to complain to politicians about COMER as judges denied trial for declaratory relief of well-past-due outdated law that continues.

My one public regret is failure to convince a politician other than past NDP Hon Jack Layton to change bank law to close the Magna Carta Loophole.

Neither federal Liberal nor provincial Conservative representative will discuss bank policy of crucial concern, or the tax-budget revenue loss problem, which I would never have figured out, was a bank system problem. Eventually, I became a bank whistleblower in 2012.

I have no regret responding to a Liberal Party request for public input to the 2017 Tax Plan. I delivered my submission to Department of Finance Consultations in September 2017. It is in the Appendices and available in English and French at, www.ourcommons.ca.

However, Prime Minister, Justin Trudeau, and Finance Minister, Bill Morneau, seemed willing to deal justice to potential criminals paying tax windfalls, rather than close the Magna Carta Loophole to save tax shortfalls.

Justice evolved that companies prepay fines to avoid trial of anticipated illicit acts with *'Remediation Deals'* also called a DPA – Deferred Prosecution Agreement.

The favor of a DPA might have saved a lot of courtroom drama and legal expense instead of 12 years in court over private and public losses in the Perris affair.

DPAs are well-established in the USA that companies and wealthy individuals prepay prosecution immunity. England and France restrict DPAs to corporations, and other countries have their own rules.

Canada included DPA Criminal Code in and among a 500 page budget Omnibus Bill that was passed into law in September, 2018.

Government agencies, municipalities, public entities, and trade unions, are not eligible for DPAs in Canada.

Liberal government timing to legalize DPAs coincided with a special effort for SNC-Lavalin; a Montreal-based company faced a federal suit that alleged some $48m in bribes to do business in Libya from 2001 to 2011.

The Public Prosecution Service refused an SNC request for a DPA in September 2018, which the company re-appealed to government to obtain in October 2018.

The law was criticized that it was hidden in the 2018 Tax Plan to avoid debate of a criminal matter in the budget that the DPA was passed into law unnoticed.

Once Parliament legalized its DPA, news followed that the Prime Minister and cabinet ministers urged former Supreme Court Justice, Jody Wilson-Raybould to use her power as Minister of Justice and Attorney General to assist SNC. The minister was pressured to persuade prosecutors to approve a DPA for the company and to shelve charges to stay public prosecution. But the Attorney General wouldn't compromise on principle as government ethics were questioned in headline news.

Prime Minister Justin Trudeau denied pressure that in his view he simply wanted law to work for a private company in the best interest of public good, which in this case was to save jobs for people in Quebec.

But the Attorney General, Jody Wilson-Raybould was against political interference in a phone call from Privy Council, Michael Wernick recorded in December, 2018 that excerpts became headline news in March 2019;

Wilson Raybould: *"This is going to look like nothing but political interference by the Prime Minister; by you, by everyone else that has been involved in... politically pressuring me into this."*

Wernick: *"[PM] wants to know why the DPA route which Parliament provided for isn't being used. And I think he is gonna find a way to get it done one way or another."*

Wilson-Raybould: *"This goes far beyond saving jobs— this is about the integrity of the Prime Minister and interference. Does [PM] understand the gravity of what this potentially could mean? This is like breaching a constitutional principle of prosecutorial independence."*

Breakdown of trust led to quitting after Jane Philpott and Jody Wilson-Raybould were moved in a cabinet shuffle. They stayed on in caucus, until they resigned to run as independents in their own ridings.

Resignations were not without intrigue— Scott Brison, left the Treasury Board, as President in January 2019, to BMO, as Vice Chairman, Investment and Corporate Business in February 2019. Attorney General Wilson-Raybould reportedly refused the bank DPA protection as lawsuits loomed from questionable business in the trans-mountain pipeline deal to carry oil from Albert to BC west coast ports across indigenous lands.

Gerald Butts, Principle Secretary to Prime Minister Justin Trudeau, and friend, who was reported to have setup the bank appointment for Brinson also quit just ahead of a House of Commons Justice Committee that tested honesty, transparency, and ethics, reported in the news in March 2019.

The Liberals had an advantage of majority government that it blocked witnesses and restricted the hearing to a short agenda. But the issue carried on in the news through August 2019 when the Ethics Commissioner, Mario Dion reported reprehensible behavior;

'The authority of the Prime Minister and his office was used to circumvent, undermine and ultimately attempt to discredit the decision of the Director of Public Prosecution as well as the authority of Ms Wilson-Raybould as the Crown's chief law officer.'

It vindicated government representatives who stood for integrity, but it was a sad comment on Prime Minister, Justin Trudeau. He said he accepted the report and he took responsibility without apology as he maintained his rule was for the common good, and he would rule the same again.

In September 2019, the Clerk of the Privy Council who serves the PMO – Prime Minister Office was in the news having decided to not lift cabinet confidentiality for an RCMP investigation that investigators may look into an obstruction of justice of a possible cover-up;

'Concealment of wrongdoing, especially by a conspiracy of deception, nondisclosure, and destruction of evidence, combined with a refusal to cooperate with investigators. A cover-up often involves obstruction of justice.'

~~~~~~~~~~~

23. Twice Paid Tax Credit Windbill Deficit Dollars

Magna Carta principle since 1215 celebrated its 800th anniversary of law denied trial for clarification in 2015.

There was no news when Justice Russell ruled against trial of Magna Carta Loophole Gullible Taxpayer Law. Judges purged my testimony as witness for COMER. And a Comer Motion to Reconsider, and to Appoint an Assessor to measure financial harm was purged from the court record January 25, 2017. It was only then that COMER was finally denied trial on May 4, 2017.

If ever one descriptor defined dream laws and politics for hungry bankers, it was *'Double-presentment'* on CBC News, on April 1, 2017. It confirmed the purpose of the bank effect of making sense fake money;

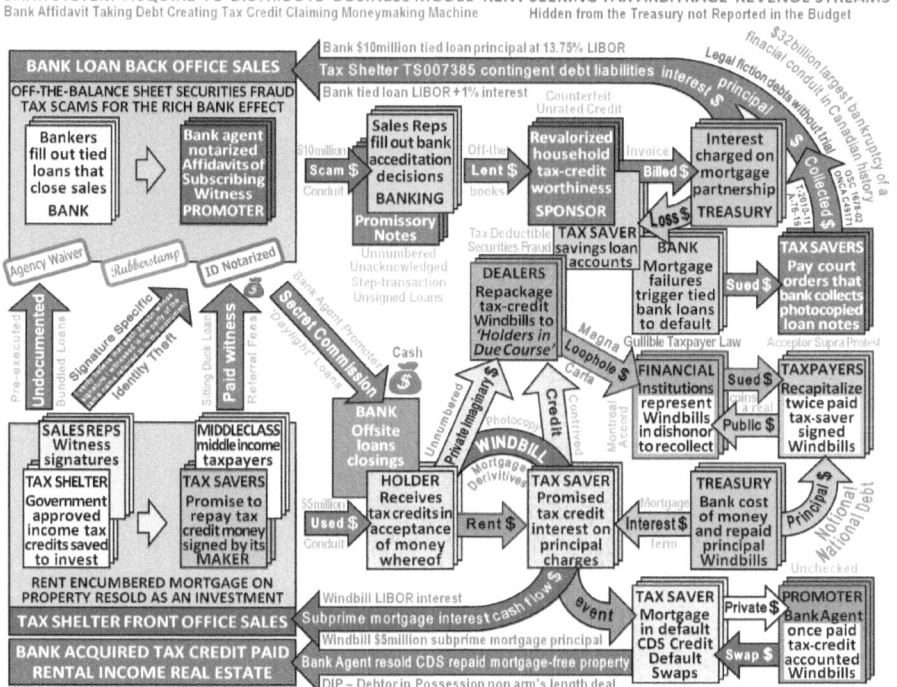

When the CBC warned the public to beware of banks that a cell-phone image of a cheque can be credited to a deposit account, from a checking account, once and twice, or more presented— it is the same as a Windbill.

Not paid once, but twice by photocopy is plain to see.

People live busy lives and have little time for hard to believe news, especially on April fool's day, but to me it was a good allegory for a conclusion in Ruly English.

For COMER a better conclusion would have been trial of the money rule of law for taxpayer protection, which our government has shown willing to override when it choses private interests over public interests not in the best interest of political ambition to be in public office.

It is history that the Minister of Justice and Attorney General was Defendant in the COMER affair. It might have been political or personal he did not intervene in concern of either private or public debt without trial. It was an ethics dilemma that the only solution was bound to be a truth embargo through justice denied.

Nothing is proven, except the law of loopification;

'In critical legal studies, the collapse of a legal distinction resulting when two ends of a continuum become so similar that they become indistinguishable. For example it may be impossible to distinguish "public" from "private"' because of loopification.

Still, I have a right to disagree, and this book offers a solution to an accounting problem that if people want a budget to balance itself— as Prime Minister Justin Trudeau once said, it would simply require a bank transaction control number to distinguish public from private money to tax, and vice versa.

That and double entry bookkeeping across the system.

Otherwise a Windbill is coined once through double-entry bookkeeping of private count in commercial and shadow bank balances, and twice through single-entry bookkeeping of public count in central bank balances. It is a well-defined practice in NOTES ON THE LAW on this book cover that people can read how billings work in Pitman's, *'Bills, Cheques, and Notes'* eBook edition, which includes the Bills of Exchange Act, 1882.

The increasing poverty gap that divides struggling law-abiding people from lawbreakers who cheat is obvious when you follow money through the triune system of central-commercial-investment bank accounts.

It has to do with the hierarchical conversion of money through triune levels of private and public exchange as it was written in the Charter for the Bank of England.

It has been some 300 years since the Bank of England reinvented money that a private Central Bank charged interest on public debt paid as rent to use convertible currency *'Banknotes'* that coined gold into the Bank until the gold standard was discontinued in 1931.

A hierarchical system supports the principle all money is a promise to pay that the most assured credit is tax Bonded to Pay Central Bank loans. Less secured is the commercial bank Promised to Pay personal credit, and least secured is Pledged to Pay invested credit used to raise capital in security agreements where there is the least regulation of the most money in investment bank system accounts.

The Public Bank of Canada issued near zero-interest cost of debt is money that the nation prospered by the economic advantage from 1933 to 1974.

Private Bank of England Gold Standard Money 1694 - 1931

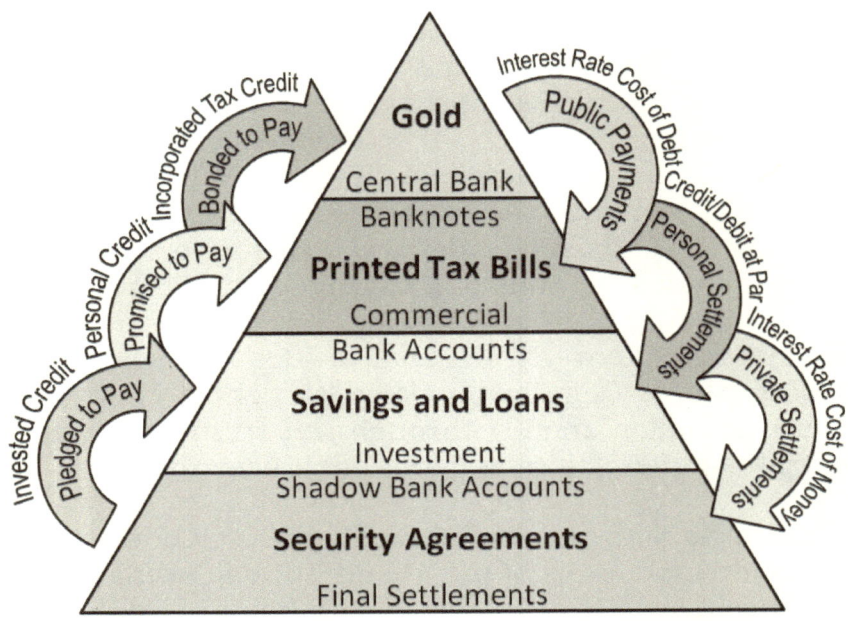

Public Bank of Canada Money 1933 - 1974

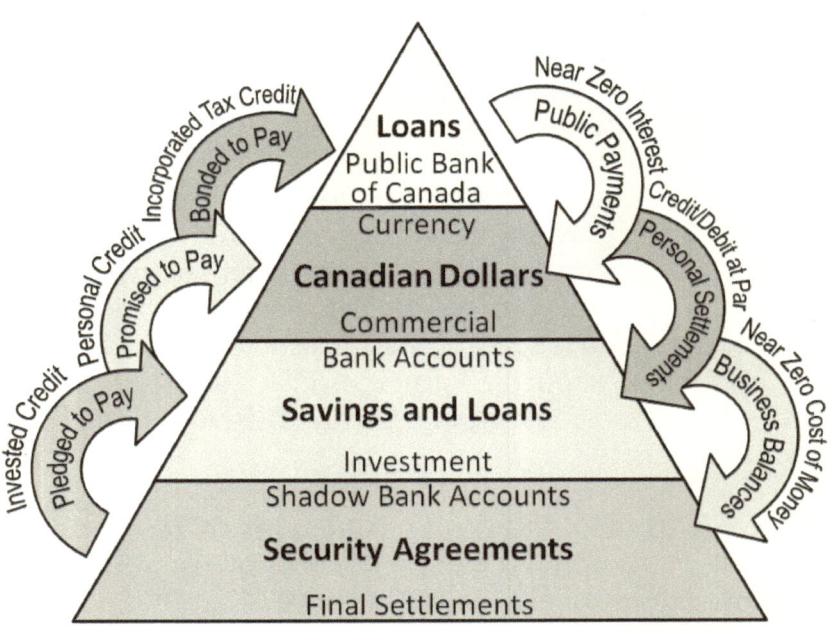

The economic advantage of a Public Bank of Canada in the Canadian Constitution to borrow its own money from national debt to print Canadian Dollars ended in 1974 when Prime Minister Pierre Elliot Trudeau chose the BIS – Bank of International Settlements to budget Public Payments to offshore loans for Printed Bills in league with members of the BIS cartel.

BIS - Bank of International Settlements Money Since 1974

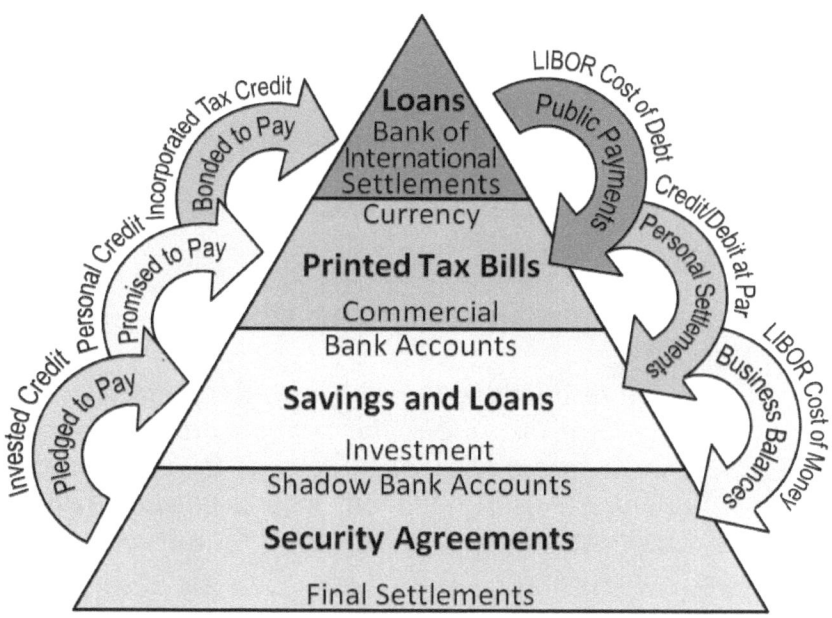

Galati made allowances that the late Prime Minister may not have known what he'd done in 1974. Lawyers said the same that judges did not understand or want my factum in court that I alleged Perris trafficked my signature from a Pledged to Pay ABCP tax-credit Note signed as a tax saver settled in Business Balances that was carried over to a Bonded to Pay ABCP tax-credit Note signed as a taxpayer suable for Public Payment, that followed a Promised to Pay ABCP bank loan Note collected Personal Settlements paid out Court Ordered debt and bank legal fees remitted in Printed Bills.

It follows that a photocopied Pledged to Pay tax-credit Windbill signed by me as the tax-saver was accounted in Final Settlements in Business Balances while the original Windbill— signed by me, as the taxpayer, was sued to reclaim from me as an *'Accommodation Party'*;

'...the person who signs the bill as drawer, acceptor, or indorser, without receiving any value therefore, for the purpose of accommodating some other person. An accommodation party is liable to a holder for value.'

It follows that Perris signed witness of me a tax-saver signing a Windbill the same person as its taxpayer set up to reconvert a second *'Presentment for Payment'*;

'...*production of an instrument to the drawee, acceptor, or maker for payment.*'

It also follows it was sued to re-collect in *'Dishonor'*;

'...*a bill is dishonoured either by non-acceptance or by non-payment. That is, where the person on whom a bill is drawn (the drawee) refuses to accept it, or where the person who by accepting the bill (the acceptor), agreed to pay it, fails to do so on the day on which it is due, the bill is said to be dishonoured.*'

For a judge to re-honor my word in *'Presentment'*;

'...*the act of presenting or laying before a court or other tribunal a formal statement about a matter to be dealt with legally.*'

Paid by me in my stead as *'Acceptor Supra Protest'*;

'...one who accepts a bill that has been protested, for the honor of the drawer or an indorser.'

~~~~~~~~~~~

24. Consumer Safeguards and Taxpayer Protection

Signature-specific-identity-theft was an election issue in 2006 in the Federal Election when party candidates answered call-in questions on television,

"Let's move on to the first call, and on the line we have Tony, go ahead with your question, please"

"Well this is about consumer protection, and a scam called 'Sitting Duck' loans that the Liberal party has promised protection on, and also opening an OSC investigation that's been quashed. The question is— If a government knew of a sleazy bank practice that tricks people into debt with tied loans based on third parties representing other peoples' signatures to link secret debts with retirement investment plans, would a government side with the banks to allow profiteering to continue, or would a government expose it and do something to protect people from a debt crisis?"

"Tony, thank you for your question. Tina Agrell," [NDP]

"Tony presented this situation to the NDP during a riding association at the beginning of December, and you may also have seen his highly visible van parked around town to publicize his indignation. As Tony described his experience of identity theft to the NDP members at the Town Restaurant, their reactions swung from initial denial— that doesn't happen in Canada surely? To doubt and then horror at the idea that yes, it could, and it probably happens more often than we realize... if it was allowed to go unchecked. Hundreds of Canadians have suddenly found them-selves responsible for millions of dollars in debt. We have to acknowledge the situation exists and then strengthen the powers of the Security Commission so that they can prevent this practice."

"Terence Young," [Conservative]

"Thank you very much. I know the gentleman who's calling; in fact I took some time, about 8 weeks ago to meet with him in his home to understand his issue and to look for potential solutions. And, I've committed if we form a government, I will meet with the new Minister of Finance and we will correct the situation and put in the legislation and stop it from happening."

"Thank you... Laura Domsy," [Green Party]

"First of all I'd just like to say— in all banks, and this is from my personal experience, because that's where I'm employed— That, if you are not following compliance and audit regulations then you are not doing your job and the bank isn't going to keep you around for a very long time. Second of all, if that is happening then I believe as soon as the government finds out about it they would put a stop to it, most definitely. And also, I think that banks have to be doing their due diligence to ensure they are knowing their customers, they know who is sitting across from them, and that they're not doing anything that has to do with tied loans, which is illegal, it's illegal to do any sort of tied selling, and I think that, yes... the government would definitely be against that... and put a stop to it, right away."

"Bonnie Brown," [Liberal]

"Thank you very much. I too am aware of Tony and his case. He has brought it to my attention. I have received all the papers that he has about his case and I have taken them to the Finance Department and I believe they ended up in the office of the Superintendent of Financial Institutions. The answer we got back over that was that nothing could be done."

The incumbent candidate was noncommittal,

"Now, the good news is that the Canadian Bankers Association has identified identity theft as one of the number one problems facing the world in this new era of the internet etc. and they have a project ongoing right now that it is trying to come up with solutions to it."

And then took it somewhat personal,

"Um, I know that Tony feels very negatively about the banks, but I think I want to say out loud that the Canadian banks are among the best in the world. Thank you."

I don't think I was negative about banks; I just wanted to resolve a problem I was still trying to understand. My representative, MP Bonnie Brown had not told me that nothing could or would be done until I heard it said on television. And so nothing was done as the tax-credit scam continued on to when the banks failed in 2008.

One of the people negative about banks was Galati.

Maybe not as negative about banks as government, but he sued the Public Bank of Canada on behalf of COMER and taxpayers for years. I would have been glad to have appeared in court as an expert witness.

I wish I could have been more help, but Ann Emmett was the only taxpayer suing for clarification of ancient law that was not forthcoming. Indeed heavily guarded that judges used Rule 74 to purge my testimony about the hierarchy of money from the court record. And the judgment of the Supreme Court of Canada to refuse an oral hearing and deny leave to appeal from the Federal Court of Appeal was final and without explanation. So, we have Magna Carta Loophole Gullible Taxpayer Law.

The alleged nefarious Ways and Means of unaccounted tax credits hidden from the Treasury not reported in the budget is NCND – Neither Confirmed Nor Denied.

Ann Emmett was a teacher, and I wish I'd been taught more about money in my youth. I underestimated the incentive of money on Perris and other CAs like him to send people into debt for secret commission tied loans that only the law makes it safe for criminals.

The Comer *'Money, Tax, and Poverty'* conference was on January 24, 2015, and COMER set up a classroom in a courtroom setting on January 26, 2015 for people to watch litigation and learn from legislation. If it had not been for Ann Emmett we would not have seen how notwithstanding removes the common right to sue, or to give evidence, to test the wisdom of outdated law.

Now we have DPA law, which even that is not enough that Parliament rules to block investigations of alleged criminal acts. In the case of tax deductible tax fraud people are overwhelmed with *'debt-is-money'* exactly as President Trump described in his inaugural address at the White House back in 2017;

"The wealth of our middleclass has been ripped from their homes and distributed all across the world. But, that is behind us and we are looking only to the future."

On September 11, 2019 Prime Minster, Justin Trudeau stood Parliament down for an election. Maybe a party would promise to restore the Bank of Canada to public use to make cheap money in the interest of Canadian taxpayers, and comply with law to keep a transparent account of tax distributions for the common good.

This book was written for whoever the party might be.

~~~~~~~~~~~

25. Magna Carta Loophole Gullible Taxpayer Law

There was no news Justice Russell ruled for the Crown that Magna Carta principle was not judiciable to try in court, ruled not a place to argue the politics of law.

And so, COMER was quietly struck down in 2017.

People in the 21st century have little understanding of money rules of law to which they're held accountable.

The gap that divides a law abiding 99% compared to 1% lawmakers whose use of law for financial gain is all too obvious. But, that is how the law is parsed today.

As ghastly as it was thinking a judge had accepted and decided upon a different factum, which was not mine, and ruled no credible evidence for trial, it was dreadful to find a NOTE DEFAULT AGAINST the Bank Agent in DEFAULT OF: Filing a Notice of Intent to Defend, and/or a Statement of Defense in another court how my lawyer blocked my way to judgment by default.

It got worse; the bank refused to clear paid writs until it extorted signed releases for itself, its own agent, and Perris. Just as Affidavits of Subscribing Witness setup loan-dependent securities fraud, a lawyer for the bank swore another Affidavit of Subscribing Witness of my signing consent to withdraw my counterclaim as long as the bank lifted a lien told to be on my house. It was before a judge in court somehow reused by the same judge at the same time with me in another court how my absence discharged my lawyer with no defense of alleged obstruction of justice by default judgment;

'Judgment entered against a defendant who has failed to plead or otherwise defend against the plaintiff's claim, often by failing to appear at trial.'

A forged signature is not an easy thing, and it used to be illegal, but a sworn Affidavit of Subscribing Witness saves time especially when its notarization lies.

An Affidavit of Subscribing Witness is a standard form that can be altered and initialed for multiple purposes, whatever witness of legal advance is required. It is a blunt instrument that can be used before or after any event, to swap any truth in fact, to any plausible lie.

I reviewed my experience of signature-specific identity theft affidavits in tax arbitrage operations behind the 2008 Global Credit Crunch. It was too complicated for me to anticipate at the time in 1989, but once I had it figured I wrote Minister of Finance, James Flaherty, in 2007 that I recommended a bank system transaction control number for revenue security, and protection.

Nothing was done and my experience was the same as COMER, except that people wanted to know about the lawsuit, which was in the news. But there was little interest in the real problem and system solution that aside from academia was rarely discussed.

The HES - History of Economics Society invited me to the June 2017 Conference at Toronto University to present, *'A Bank System Solution to Improperly Earned Income Tax Credits and Twice Paid Tax Credit Windbill Conversions'* paper. My lengthy subtitle described the content, *'A study of the Asset Backed Commercial Paper ABCP 'Crisis in Canada' twice paid tax credit ABCP Windbill theory that Canadian taxpayers need more protection than US Improper Payments Elimination and Recovery Act, 2010, provides.'*

That was 2017, and I was invited to speak more about my research topic of twice-paid tax-credit Windbills as I responded to more calls for papers in 2018.

I described a Poster Presentation at the 2018 FINEXUS Conference at the University of Zurich and gave an ABCNotes socioeconomic prototype tutorial for INET at the Trento University, Italy, 2018 Festival Economia.

Asset Backed Commercial Notes – ABCNotes includes Ruly English structure to check for proper grammar demonstrated in my paper, *'Socioeconomic Prototype Gap Analysis of Finance Law and Economics'*.

The academic paper reviewed socioeconomic system gap analysis of finance, law, and economics factored in words of accountability, uniformity and responsibility that reenacted fiscal, legal, and surety concerns. Policy lines of control for regulation, and enforcement replayed triple relationships of dataflow, workflow, and cash flow interactions in the context of oversight, inequality and noncompliant outcomes in various cases of process redesign, and new technology issues.

It was a coincidence that the CBC reported a modern bank-system *'Double Presentment'* technology problem on April 1, 2018.

The CBC program warned that bank-checking account holders must double-check for multiple-photocopied deposits as Canadian banks were no longer held responsible for the validity of how cheques are received in due course.

So there it was, not exactly telling people the law, that a bank is always right in section 165(3), repeated here for those who might think of technology the problem;

'Where a cheque is delivered to a bank for deposit to the credit of a person and the bank credits him with the amount of the cheque, the bank acquires all the rights and powers of a holder in due course of the cheque.

I used the GoPublic bank system scenario to prototype a socioeconomic situation of bank law how cell-phone image technology bypasses zero-balanced banking that used to be manual before computers were invented.

A triune system fails to prevent fraud when regulation and enforcement of bank system inputs and outputs connect across separate work-tray processes. The rule of bank law allows multiple arrivals of duplicate photocopied cheques to deposit on account puts the burden of proof of error on the client, not the bank.

I presented Ruly English methodology in context of a *'Double Presentment'* problem of multiple deposits of identical cheques copied into one account. The study objective was for student participation in a workshop setting to locate double credit/debit bank payment events and to recommend a *'Block Chain'* system-like solution through methodological process gap analysis.

Students reviewed Ruly English that words described distortion, disconnection, and disruption outcomes of accountability, uniformity, and responsibility that the design flaw could be traced back to section 165(3) law.

The class solved the problem that a bank transaction control number would pre-check a multiple payment of photographed images of cheques on account.

We discussed several examples of *'Double Presentment'* financial losses and my paper included a Ruly English Magna Carta Loophole Gullible Taxpayer Law scenario that tracks photocopied bills in two financial markets.

I enjoyed the opportunity for discussion and an INET YSI – Young Scholars Initiative continued to work on transparency that I felt comfortable to write my MPP about tax-credit losses due to *'Double Presentment'*.

MPP Stephen Crawford
2318 Lakeshore Road West
Oakville, ON, L6L 1H3

August 9, 2018

Dear Mr Crawford,

Subject: Private Members Bill for a Bank Transaction Number in the Tax System [1]
Ref: CBC New *'When banks cash your same cheque twice, you may be on the hook to pay'* [2]

We write about a Bank Transaction Control Number solution to the Bills of Exchange Act, 1882, failure to regulate criminal double-deposit photocopied bills, cheques, and notes in Canadian credit markets.

In April 2018, CBC GoPublic News warned people beware *'Smartphone'* MBA – Mobile Banking Apps that photocopied deposits multiply cheque repayments through double presentments. A signed cheque image, which is an *'Unsigned Draft'*, is transmitted by RDC– Remote Deposit Capture to a BoFD – Bank of First Deposit as well as real *'Signed Deposit'* original note. Payments Canada encourages paperless banking that half of the 800 million cheques transacted last year were photo-images. The government advises consumers check statements, not banks, to flag double-billing. It warns 400 million people to check personal bank statements for the so-called *'Fictitious Bill'* to ensure they don't end up, quote; *"Paying double, for cheques they have written"*.

It was not until April 1, 2018 when GoPublic reported seventeen presentments of a cheque that a Canadian bank acknowledged the problem to reverse the bank-technology credit-to-debit double-billing machine.

Double presentment multiplies as many single-entry-double-booked credits for as much zero-balanced double entry credit-debit worth launders reimaged signed promises to pay money from credit in bank accounts.

But, single-entry-double-booked credit in double-entry-credit-debit bookkeeping to defraud is nothing new. The Bills of Exchange Act, 1882, predates photocopies that double-booked credit paid from duplication was a counterfeit, or a confidence trick, in breach of coded ways and means of Windbill law defined in the Act.

Canadian judges rule photocopied signed promises to pay money from credit are not forgeries, but legal and properly documented bank transactions. They accepted them as signed bills, cheques, and notes that a promise *'Maker'* owes value to a *'Holder'*, even in the hands of a thief, which is the double-presentment moral hazard.

The bank effect of double presentment is contingent liability to a reimaged unnumbered private bill.

An unnumbered double-booked bill does not register in a credit rating system, nor does a double-booked tax credit hidden from the Treasury not reported in the budget. The *'Acquire to Distribute'* bank effect in the 2009 *'Crisis in Canada'* Report [3] estimates $85billion private and $32billion public court reordered debt collection due to double-billed twice-paid-tax-credit Windbill Third Party Notes at personal and taxpayer expense.

The bank effect of double-presentment double-billed personal credit dependent tax credit derivatives traded in two financial markets at the same time is contingent liability to reimaged unnumbered private and public bills.

Given Payments Canada warns responsibility to flag double-deposits, and personal liability to repay double-presentment double-booked credit from private bank accounts, it follows government agencies should double-check double-presentments to prevent double booked tax credits laundered for cash through the tax system.

I discussed tax law with Finance Minister, late James Flaherty that he promised me he would criminalize identity theft in 2008. However, Justice Russell ruled against a declaratory judgment of law in 2017 that multibillion tax dollar paid interest on tax credit principal losses requires political remedy, rather than legal clarification.

Specifically, we require you to table a Private Member Bill for a universal bank transaction control number that NDP, late Jack Layton signed Petition 44 and MPP Andrea Horwath read in Queen's Park Legislature in 2009 for a public inquiry for financial consumer safeguards and taxpayer protection.

Yours truly,

Jill and Tony Crawford

[1] http://www.ourcommons.ca/Content/Committee/421/FINA/Brief/BR9130835/br-external/CrawfordAnthony-e.pdf

[2] April 1, 2018. http://www.cbc.ca/news/business/duplicate-deposits-mobile-chequing-banks-1.4584304

[3] file:///C:/Users/Owner/Desktop/HES%20June%2022%202017%20Conference/The%20ABCP%20Crisis%20in%20Canada%20-%20Chant.English.pdf

My wife and I delivered a letter to my MPP at his office where we asked him to support a Private Members Bill to resolve the issue. We never heard from him again.

There was another 2019 INET Call for Papers and the YSI Finance Law and Economics Group displayed my Magna Carta Loophole Gullible Taxpayer Law poster to discuss at the University of Southern California.

Poster presentations are quicker for people to discuss complex subject matters, especially to get down to the issue and problem resolution in a bottom line;

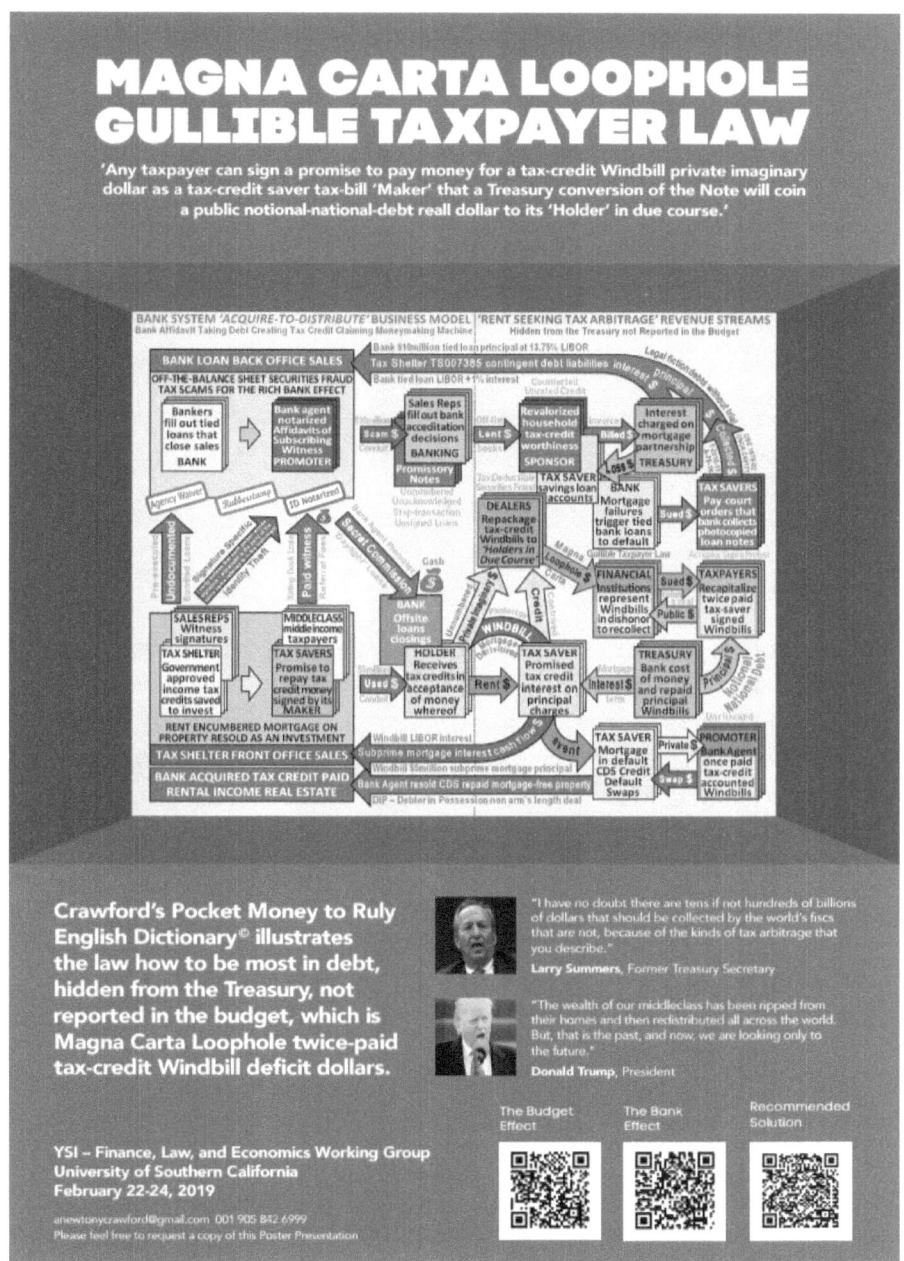

I positioned ABCP Cash Flow analysis in the center of my Magna Carta Gullible Taxpayer Law poster. ABCP color-coded cash flow is as easy to follow as a subway map of accountability, transparency and independence as COMER sued for clarification, denied trial in 2017.

The poster promoted my Pocket Money to Ruly English Dictionary with links to web page further reading, and quotes from Larry Summers and Donald Trump.

My Magna Carta Loophole Gullible Taxpayer Law poster has all the elements of content, starting with a title of principle in Ruly English law already accepted in the 2017 Tax Plan from my submission;

"Any taxpayer can sign a promise to pay money for a tax-credit Windbill private imaginary dollar as a tax-credit saver tax-bill 'Maker' that a Treasury conversion of the Note will coin a public notional national debt real dollar to its 'Holder' in due course."

When people came to see my poster I read the title and words of Crawford's law that followed bank-workflow to my tax-credit promise to carry a Windbill in private cash flow— then the rest of the lie to repay the same tax-credit amount in public cash flow with the court-ordered debt from double presentment;

'...the act of presenting or laying before a court or other tribunal a formal statement about a matter to be dealt with legally.' [10]

~~~~~~~~~~~

---

[10] Ref: Black's Law Page 1303. Presentment: formal production of a negotiable instrument for acceptance or payment. Also termed, presentation. [Cases; Bills and Notes]. Delivery of a document to an issuer or named person for the purpose of initiating action under a letter of credit.

26. Taxpayer Signed Letters of Credit

Lawyers told me it would be cathartic for me to keep a diary of courtroom experience to write a book. I didn't know it would be a cautionary tale how a bank and its agent Perris connived to contrive financial instruments from a gullible taxpayer like me. It was years before I discovered I had been tricked to sign a letter of credit beholding the Public Purse to double up private debt;

'(17c) Commercial law. An instrument under which the issuer (usually a bank), at a customer's request, agrees to honor a draft or other demand for payment made by a third party (the beneficiary), as long as the draft or demand complies with specified conditions, and regardless of whether any underlying agreement between the customer and the beneficiary is satisfied.'

Bank law is such a crafty thing I was smitten to study its art and expression in legalese; I wanted my posters to announce my dictionary;

'Crawford's Pocket Money to Ruly English Dictionary of law how to be most in debt, hidden from the Treasury, not reported in the budget, which is Magna Carta Loophole twice-paid tax-credit Windbill deficit dollars.'

I would have preferred to have continued my research in a university setting, but that fell away in the school-of-hard-knocks as lawyers pursued the law for years. Canadians heard about the Magna Carta issue from Rocco Galati for COMER when Ann Emmett sued to restore the Bank of Canada to its original purpose as a public bank. Galati told the story on the radio that Prime Minister, Pierre Elliot Trudeau had given the economic advantage of it away in 1974.

Trillions of dollar losses have never been denied.

Judges won't hear testimony about the budget process that constitutional lawyer Rocco Galati alleged illegal acts presented in court for trial of apparent tort. And, Prime Minister Justin Trudeau won't discuss assumed losses, which he simply fended as conspiracy theory.

Nobody denied my bank whistleblower testimony that my tax folly centered on my signing a letter of credit;

'A credit is an original undertaking by one party (the issuer) to substitute his financial strength for that of another (the account party), with that undertaking to be triggered by the presentation of a draft or demand for payment and, often, other documents. The credit arises in a number of situations, but generally the account party seeks the strength of the issuer's financial integrity or reputation so that a third party (the beneficiary of the credit) will give value to the account party.' [11]

The trouble is that an Affidavit of Subscribing Witness cosigned the issuer and account party as one person behind double presentment of a financial instrument for two payments in private and public bank balances.

It has been 25 years since I observed the issue in the 1994 Committee Finance Report in my complaint that the bank design flaw is geared to confiscate wealth.

Those who profit by it don't see it as their problem.

Tax deductible tax fraud is quite unmentionable and often ridiculed as conspiracy theory by those who will not talk about it. That was bank defense to avoid trial for COMER and the economy became an even bigger issue after 2019 Election than it ever was before. That and climate change.

---

[11] Black's Law Page 987, John F. Dolan, The Law of Letters of Credit (1984).

The 2019 election added more parties that promised tax savings to largely undecided voters polled at 32% for Liberal and Conservative, 20% NDP, 7% BQ – Bloc Québécois, 6% Green Party, 1% PP – People's Party, all of it trending towards a minority government.

All the parties promoted financial incentives to combat climate change including Liberal carbon tax geared to price emission offset to reductions saved on account. Conservative policy was to scrap the tax and force big polluters to invest in emission reducing technology.

The Liberal platform was for more tax on the superrich and less tax on the middleclass, and more spending to invest in Canada. The Conservative platform was lower taxes on wages and austerity cutbacks to balance the budget and an inquiry into the SNC-Lavalin affair. The NDP planned universal pharmacare, dental coverage, mental health, addiction services, vision, and hearing. The NDP also positioned itself as a tiebreaker in favor of a joint Liberal minority government.

All the parties announced traditional tax-rate-adjusted revenue redistribution policy with one exception: The Green Party also promised a tax on bank transactions and closing a $15billion corporate-tax loophole to fund post-secondary education from recovered revenue.

Closing tax loopholes is a Liberal government priority to collect more revenue through tax returns. But eliminating a shortfall for an immediate $15billion benefit is an entirely different math. It requires a bank control number at the accounting level to tax financial transactions, which I recommended in my submission to the 2017 Tax Plan in this book still pending review.

The 2019 Federal Election returned a minority Liberal government to Prime Minister Justin Trudeau.

The Liberal campaign had started badly with criticism the Prime Minister hassled former Attorney General, Jody Wilson Raybould, to grant a *'Remediation Deal'* to SNC-Lavalin to avoid corruption charges. The Ethics Commissioner ruled Trudeau acted improperly having had her demoted in a cabinet shuffle and dismissed for upholding the Magna Carta principle of law.

SNC-Lavalin battered the Prime Minister in the news since April 2019 that while Justin Trudeau was never shy to apologize for past crimes of the nation he would not accept blame or admit wrongdoing in breaking the law. The former Attorney General ran for election as an Independent in the Vancouver BC, Granville riding.

The Conservative platform promised an inquiry of the SNC-Lavalin affair and giving more power to the ethics committee and steeper fines for breaches of law.

The campaign started on political issues but morphed to personal matters as the news released photographs of Justin Trudeau in stereotypical dark-face mimicry of visible minorities, but he admitted to inappropriate behavior, and that he should have known better.

Time Magazine bared Prime Minister Justine Trudeau soul as a sorry figure in the world on its front cover. He apologized for weeks in a roundabout way that all Canadians must learn from his contrition.

The election result was more about losses than gains.

Liberals won 156, Conservatives 122, BQ 32, NDP 24, Green 3, Independent 1, and PP 0 seats. BQ gains on Liberal losses backed the NDP into a balance of power fourth place that even with sizable losses; it celebrated the final vote as if it had won a national mandate to align with a Liberal Party ruling coalition.

On October 23, 2019, Prime Minister Justin Trudeau stood in the National Press Theatre where he spoke to his minority mandate. He had 20 fewer seats in 2019 than 2015, but he ruled out coalition, and he offered to work with all Canadians to save the environment.

Electioneering tends to avoid real debate of real issues. The Prime Minister was mum the judiciary had ruled out trial of alleged government breach of Magna Carta, *'no taxation without representation'* principle,

"I think there were a lot of issues that weren't properly addressed. I think there were big, substantive ideas that weren't fully debated in this election campaign, and I regret that. I recognize that much of this campaign tended to be around me, and I do hold a bit of responsibility for that. But, this Parliament and this government will be, and needs to be focused on Canadians. And that means we need to work together. We need to listen to each other. We need to figure out the right way forward for every part of the country. And that is something I am committed to doing."

The Prime Minister focused on moving forward,

"Moving forward on Child Benefit that lifted thousands of people out of poverty, particularly kids, moving forward on the national housing strategy, moving forward on lowering tax for the middleclass and raising them for the wealthiest one percent, these are all things upon which there would be broad consensus in the House or a positive consensus from progressive parties."

And that his first priority was a bill for tax reform,

"I expect them to be able to vote with us on things like the very first we'll do, which will be to put forward a bill on lower taxes for the middleclass."

Justin Trudeau might expect the House to vote for less tax on the middleclass, except for lingered doubt.

There could be an inquiry; Conservatives still question public influenced private deals. The Greens still want to tax bank transactions and close tax loopholes. The Independent representative chiefly wants law abiding government. And, people are mostly concerned about Mother Nature, on the brink of default of used credit in an economic system that monetizes everything.

Swedish activist Greta Thunberg said as much at the 2019 United Nations Climate Action Summit,

"We are at the beginning of mass extinction, and all you can talk about is money and fairy tales of eternal economic growth."

They won't link money to climate change, she said,

"...they change the subject every time the climate crisis comes up."

It was the same in the Occupy movement in 2011. Not many linked law to economics except in Canada in the COMER lawsuit for judgment to clarify the law.

The case before the court concerned tax redistribution from the budget process. Indeed the real reason for the Constitutional Challenge was to check the bank effect of unequal shares of most welfare to the one percent.

The judiciary is the only institution that <u>must</u> act to protect the law, which is ever more difficult as it must be independent of control by certain individuals to be still respected by taxpayers. People feel victimized by corporate anti-system and pro-chaos approaches to deregulation that impinges on rights and freedoms.

There was a time in the 1300s when judges declared *"Don't tell us the law, we wrote it!"* It established a precedent to manipulate the law for unjust purposes.

Contested values in society follow rules of law, which is the doctrine that judicial process must be exercised to protect the law. Any inequity in law will be resolved in due course— in the fullness of time.

William Krehm, Ann Emmett, and Canadian taxpayers were denied trial in 2017. The former governor of the Bank of Canada, Mark Carney, did not have to testify in court what he privately admits and warns in public,

"The challenges currently posed by climate change pale in significance compared with what might come. Once climate change becomes a defining issue for financial stability, it may already be too late." [12]

The monitory does not bode well for sustainability.

Environmentalists want governments to bill science in Acts of Law to protect the ecosystem for living things. They question the theory of regulating the economy by varying the amount and rate of money in circulation is not real science. Especially, the math of infinite growth is not possible in a finite system which is Planet Earth.

A bank is always right— section 165(3) could be wrong.

Indeed, COMER claimants questioned the wisdom of <u>not</u> revealing a true account of tax-credit deficit dollars in the budget as banks, courts, and governments still condone Magna Carta Loophole Gullible Taxpayer Law.

Conventional wisdom says banks are too big to fail.

---

[12] University of Zurich FINEXUS Conference 2018: Financial Sustainability.

But the bank effect of making sense fake money billing tax credit paper to collect twice over is a moral hazard, "hazard that has its inception in mental attitudes, such as dishonesty, carelessness , and insanity."[1]

Section 165(3) provides legal right for a bank to plead its own wrongdoing in defense of actual misconduct. Justice Russell opposed trial for COMER and advised taxpayers complain to lawmakers to change the law.

On December 5, 2019, Governor General, Julie Payette announced Liberal government priorities to lower tax for the middleclass and to combat money laundering.

But it's not likely. The taxpayer proposed Class Action denied trial for clarification of Magna Carta Loophole Gullible Taxpayer Law was sued in last resort. Prime Minister Justin Trudeau doesn't believe in conspiracy, the same as the bank said in court to avoid trial in the Perris affair. There is no honor in court endorsed cons who continue to defraud taxpayers by design, and my OSC Whistleblower file is still pending restitution.[2]

Socioeconomic prototype analysis for academic review of Ruly English bank design in ABCNotes[3] was denied trial by Superior, Appeal, and Supreme Court judges. I swore it in truth, but they all refused to judge it.

This volume was not easy, Canadian skeptics say, "It's only in the USA." In which case, President Trump may be the only honest tax-credit billionaire to promise tax reform in return for taxpayer votes to change tax law.

~~~~~~~~~~~

---

[1] www. blacks-law-dictionary-9th-edition.pdf. Page 786 Hazard Insured
[2] OSC Whistleblower Act. Crawford Submission October 31, 2017
[3] Trento University May 2018: Disruptive Technologies Inequalities and Law.

Section 165(3) Cheque Conversion System Analysis

Ten-Step Double Presentment Twice Paid Tax Credit Windbill Workflow

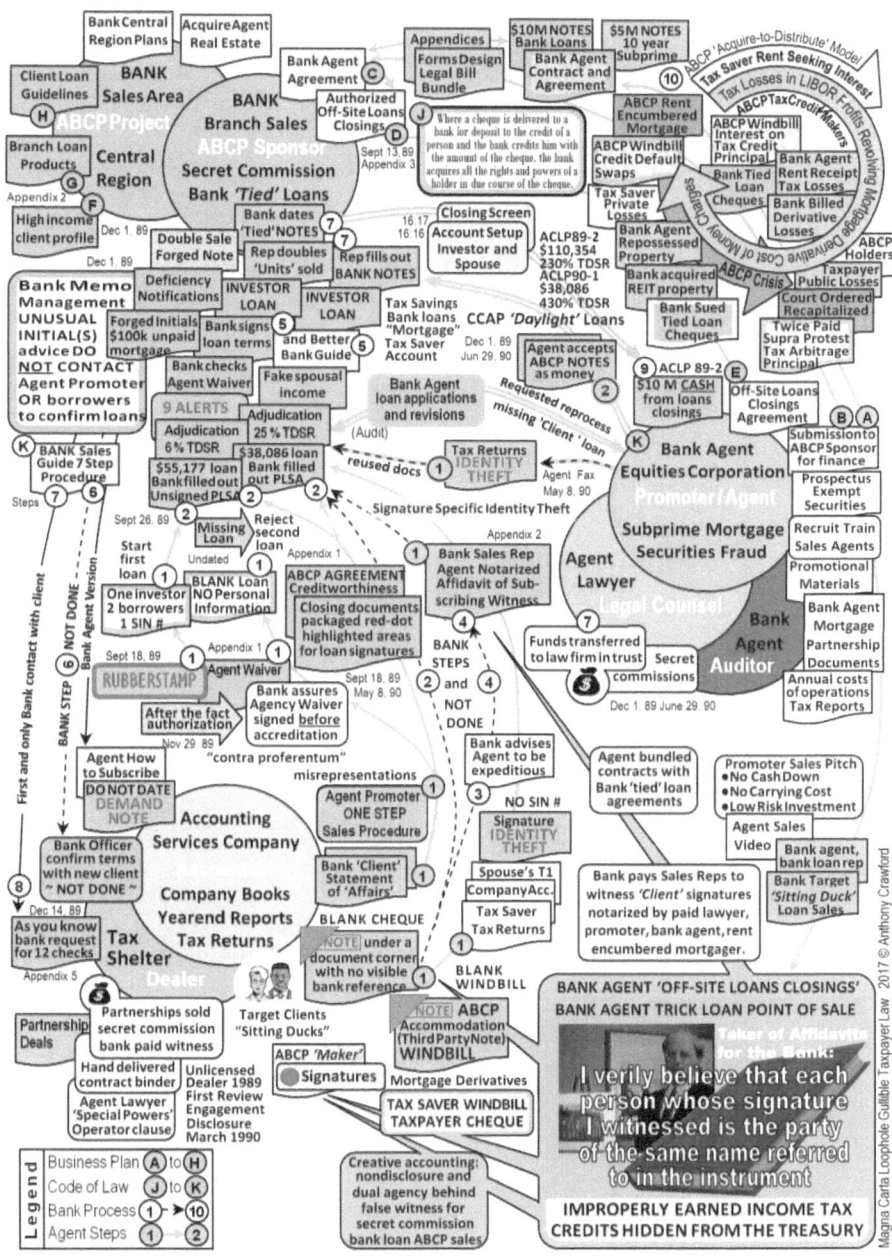

27. Crawford Submission to the 2017 Tax Plan

Anthony Crawford of Oakville Submission to Department of Finance's Consultations September 29, 2017

http://www.ourcommons.ca/Content/Committee/421/FINA/Brief/BR9130835/br-external/CrawfordAnthony-e.pdf

Title: The Magna Carta Loophole

Subtitle: Bank System Solution to Twice Paid Tax Credit Windbill Conversions

This Magna Carta Loophole essay describes how bank principles monetize tax scams for the rich. It refers to the Asset Backed Commercial Paper – ABCP conversion problem that Canadian taxpayers need more protection than income tax code adjustments provide.

Briefly, the Twice-Paid-Tax-Credit-Windbill, described from bank dictionaries, is a tax scam that defrauds income tax-credit savers of private wealth and taxpayer expenditures of public wealth using the same tax credit unnumbered financial instrument to profit in different capital markets, at the same time.

Canadian financial analyses circa 1990 estimated tax-shelters reduced Canadian revenue some $8 billion each year. [13]

> **WINDBILL** *Windmill, names sometimes given to accommodation bills;* [14]

> **ACCOMMODATION BILL** *a bill of exchange endorsed by a reputable third party (called an accommodation party) acting as a guarantor, as a favor and without compensation. The bill then can be discounted on the financial strength of the guarantor who remains liable until the bill [tax bill] is paid. Also called accommodation note, accommodation paper, or (in the UK) Windbill;* [15]

---

[13] Ref: William Krehm. A Power Unto Itself. Page 41, Neil Brooks, a tax specialist at Osgoode Hall Law School, has estimated that the government loses $8 billion in revenue to questionable tax shelters every year.

[14] Ref: R. W. Jones, Thomson's Dictionary of Banking, New Era Publishing WINDBILLS, WINDMILLS Page 656.

[15] Ref: Business Dictionary
http://www.businessdictionary.com/definition/accommodation-bill.html

FICTITIOUS BILL *'accommodation bills' also known as 'fictitious bills,' 'kites,' and 'windmills' and the persons who draw, accept, or indorse them are called 'accommodation parties'.* [16]

President Trump with a billion income tax credit deficit dollars avoided paying Federal income tax some twenty years, and he said:

"The wealth of our middle-class has been ripped from their homes and been redistribute all across the world." [17]

This Windbill analysis is based on the 2009 Government of Canada commissioned ABCP 'Crisis in Canada' Report by Prof John Chant of Simon Fraser University. [18] Prof Chant defines the $112billion ABCP 'Acquire-to-Distribute' business model behind the 2008 Global Credit Crunch largest $32billion bankruptcy of a financial conduit in Canadian history. And, Prof Larry Summers, President, Harvard University former US Treasury Secretary keynote addressed the 2014 Toronto Institute of New Economic Thinking – INET Conference about the *'Dark Side of Capital Mobility'* concerning hundreds of billions of uncollected tax dollars in world fiscs:

PROF LARRY SUMMERS, *"The American journalist Mike Kinsley put forth the doctrine that the real scandal isn't usually the illegal things people do, it's the things that are fully legal. And that is certainly true with respect to tax sheltering and overseas tax sheltering and tax sheltering by financial institutions. Tax shelters, tax arbitrage comes in forms that are mind numbingly complex. But, its essence is that you borrow money and you deduct the interest on your borrowing and you put the money somewhere where you earn interest and you don't pay tax on the interest you earn. And, if you do those two things at the same rate and you can subtract you recognize you make a profit that's equal to the tax rate times the interest rate on each dollar of your money. And, there's no question that there's a lot of that that goes on. There's no question that but for successful rent seeking in individual countries there would be substantially less of it. There's no question that to fully address it would require more international*

---

[16] Ref: Pitmans' Bills, Cheques, and Notes, 1907. Accommodation Bills, Fictitious Bills Page 28
[17] ABC 15 Arizona News www.youtube.com/watch?v=Irrd10JjkBA
[18] Government of Canada study of the ABCP – Asset Backed Commercial Paper C$32 billion largest bankruptcy of a financial conduit in Canadian history by Professor John Chant of Simon Fraser University, BC, for the 'Expert Panel on Securities Regulation'.

cooperation than we have now. And, there's no question that it is a very serious problem, as I tried to convey when I spoke about the dark side of capital mobility. I have no doubt there are tens if not hundreds of billions of dollars that should be collected by the world's fiscs [19] *that are not, because of the kinds of tax arbitrage activities that you describe."* [20]

The issue of hundreds of billions of revenue losses monetized for cash through taxation was described as a financial miracle to those on the profit side of the tax-deductible-rental-income capital loss:

Prof Tyson *"There is money involved. From a business point of view, why shouldn't lawyers, accountants and bankers try to make money? Taxpayers were allowed to apply losses from passive investments, like limited partner-ships, to offset large amounts of ordinary income from other sources. Using depreciation, investors could claim losses on investments that actually produced profits. The basis model involves limited partnerships that invested in assets like apartment complexes. Rental income would be more than offset by operating expenses, interest on the loan and depreciation, creating a loss the partners could use to eliminate tax on tens of thousands of dollars in other income. After five years, the complex would be sold at a profit. This is what I used to call a miracle."* [21]

The US Senate Permanent Subcommittee on Investigations questioned the legality of *'Rent Seeking Tax Arbitrage'* schemes in 2005, reported and defined as follows:

"Limited partnerships invested in assets like apartment complexes. Rental income would be more than offset by operating expenses, interest on the loan and depreciation, creating a loss partners could use to eliminate tax on tens of thousands of dollars in other income. After five years, the complex would be sold at a profit."

---

[19] Ref Dictionary: Fisc n pl.–s a state or royal treasury. Ref: Webster's Dictionary. Fiscal adj. of or pertaining to the public treasury or revenue: Ref: Collin's Dictionary. Note: (Scotland) Fiscal n. treasurer, one who prosecutes for the Crown minor criminal cases.

[20] Ref: INET/CIGI Toronto Human After All Conference April 2014. Larry Summers address 'Secular Stagnation' April 12, 2014.

[21] Ref: Knowledge@Wharton Tax Shelters: Exotic or Just Plain Illegal? Miracle Workers Page 2

"The line between proper and improper shelters is so unclear that the IRS uses terms like 'abusive' to characterize unacceptable shelters rather than calling them 'illegal'. But in a 2005 study, the Senate Permanent Subcommittee on Investigations described abusive shelters as 'transactions in which a significant purpose is the avoidance or evasion of federal, state or local tax in a manner not intended by the law.'" [22]

RENT SEEKING *n. the act of trying to improve personal income at the expense of someone else, rather than by increased work or productivity. This is a term used by some economists to describe the processes through which individuals and corporations seek to use government to further their own interests and, in particular, to acquire streams of money (rents),* [23]

TAX ARBITRAGE *trading that takes advantage of a difference in tax rates or tax systems as the basis for profit,* [24]

ARBITRAGE *n. (commerce), the buying of goods in one place in order to sell them immediately in another at a higher price, the buying of bills of exchange or stocks and shares for the same purpose.* [25]

In Canada, the tax-credit cost of money was challenged in 2011 in the Federal Court of Canada that ruled against trial of an estimated trillion dollar cost of money behind doubtful income tax credits. The ruling questions the wisdom of Parliament using paying LIBOR for offshore bank loans to print onshore money instead of near zero Public Bank of Canada cost of money for earned income tax credits [26] and Court refers taxpayers to Members of Parliament to engage in public debate of government policy.

---

[22] Ref: http://knowledge.wharton.upenn.edu/article.cfm?articleid=1419 Tax Shelters: Exotic or Just Plain Illegal? Miracle Workers
[23] Ref: Dictionary Central http://www.dictionarycentral.com/definition/rent-seeking.html
[24] Ref: The Free Dictionary: Tax Arbitrage. http://financial-dictionary.thefreedictionary.com/Tax+Arbitrage
[25] Ref: Webster's Dictionary 1988 Encyclopedic Edition. ARBITRAGE Page 47.
[26] William Krehm Verses The Bank of Canada. Federal Court of Canada File T-2010-11

The Canadian Auditor General is the Accountant who reviews the government's books. In his 1993 annual report he acknowledged that most of the government's debt consisted of interest charges. Thus in 1993, 91 percent of debt consisted of interest charges, the government would have a debt of only C$37 billion ($37,000,000,000) – very low and sustainable, just as it was before 1974. By 2012, the government had paid C$1 trillion ($1,000,000,000,000) in interest – twice its national debt... [27]

The lower the interest rate cost of money before the 2008 crash – the less the impact of income tax-credit revenue shortfalls. Canadian rent-seeking tax arbitrage would have been less profitable than bank rigged LIBOR interest rates that maximized returns, as follows;

LIBOR – *London Interbank Offered Rate: the average interest rate estimated by leading banks in London that they would be charged if borrowing from other banks. LIBOR is widely used as a reference rate for many financial instruments in both financial markets and commercial fields around the world. In June 2012, multiple criminal settlements by Barclays Bank revealed significant fraud and collusion by member banks connected to the rate submission, leading to the LIBOR scandal.* [28]

My so-called *'Magna Carta Loophole Case Before the Court'* is based on the 1215 *'No Taxation Without Representation'* principle that the 1694 Bank of England followed government policy to print money capitalized from the incorporated net worth of taxpayers bonded into service the tax-credit national debt cost of money behind the first private bank public deficit economy in the world.

The medieval bank system plan replaced tax paid tally-stick receipt interest free currency with tax in trust to collect for a private bank that printed signed promises to pay pound coins for pound notes that charged the rent interest public cost of money for unpaid tax bills as Bills of Exchange to use as legal tender.

Signed promises to pay money for Bank of England banknotes circulated through countrywide bank cash flows that coined gold standard

---

[27] Ref: Ellen Brown, The Public Bank Solution. Third Millennium Press, 2013, Gross Canadian Federal Government debt 1867-2008. "From Sustainable to Unsustainable Debt." Page 207.
[28] Ref: Ellen Brown, The Public Bank Solution. Third Millennium Press, 2013, Glossary. LIBOR Page 433.

fractional reserve capital movements through the bank system and revenue streams in tax budget accounts. Even today, government throne speeches still announce election promises in budgets after tax returns to public wealth that *'Bond'* issues of unpaid tax bills continue in cash flows as money in circulation in deficit economies.

Real economy collective principle a central bank holds a social lien on national debt tax-value received is not the same as shadow banking Windbills, which are spiritual liens on notional debt-value deceived to raise credit on counterfeit, nothing received.

Tax-credit Windbills garnish gullible taxpayer income tax deductions that monetize fixed papered interest charged for Windbills laundered for cash through tax avoidance revenue shortfalls that conceal tax evasion public debt Treasury losses not reported in the budget.

Tax deductible Windbills yield interest until indebted Windbill *'Makers'* repay principal owed that nothing received to receipt Windbill *'Holders'* re-present signed promises to re-sue payment of private notional debt re-billed as public national debt re-coined from Treasury losses, which is down to Gullible Taxpayer Law:

"Any taxpayer can sign a promise to pay money for a tax credit Windbill private imaginary dollar as a tax credit saver tax bill 'Maker' that a Treasury conversion reissues a public notional national debt real dollar to its 'Holder' in due course."

Neither the 1215 Magna Carta nor the 1882 Bills of Exchange Act defines law for bank control and in 2016 the Federal Court of Canada ruled against trial of tax arbitrage that the government still issues tax credits to financial institutions that profit from financial ruin and notional national debt.

TAX LOOPHOLE, LOOPHOLE *an ambiguity, omission, or exception (as in a law or other legal document) that provides a way to avoid a rule without violating its literal requirements; especially, a tax-code provision that allows a taxpayer to legally avoid or reduce income taxes,* [29]

---

[29] Ref: Black's Law Dictionary Ninth Edition, LOOPHOLE Page 1028.

Présentation d'Anthony Crawford d'Oakville pour les consultations du ministère des Finances le 29 septembre 2017

http://www.noscommunes.ca/Content/Committee/421/FINA/Brief/BR91 30835/br-external/CrawfordAnthony-f.pdf

Objet: La planification fiscale à l'aide de sociétés privées
Référence: Contributions aux consultations du ministère des Finances

Titre : L'échappatoire de la Magna Carta

Sous-titre: Solution systémique des banques aux conversions des effets de complaisance pour crédits d'impôt payés deux fois

Cette présentation qui porte sur l'échappatoire de la Magna Carta décrit de quelle façon les principes bancaires monétisent les stratagèmes fiscaux au bénéfice des riches. Il porte notamment sur le problème de la conversion du papier commercial adossé à des actifs (PPAC) pour lequel les Canadiens ont besoin d'une protection plus forte que celle offerte par les rajustements apportés au code des impôts sur le revenu.

En bref, tels qu'ils sont décrits dans les lexiques bancaires, les effets de complaisance pour crédits d'impôt payés deux fois constituent une fraude fiscale, d'une part, à l'égard du patrimoine privé des épargnants qui bénéficient d'un crédit d'impôt et, d'autre part, à l'égard du patrimoine public formé par les contribuables. Cette fraude repose sur l'utilisation du même instrument financier de crédit d'impôt non numéroté en vue de la réalisation de bénéfices dans différents marchés financiers.

Selon les analyses financières canadiennes effectuées vers les années 1990, les abris fiscaux réduisent les revenus du Canada de près de huit milliards de dollars par année [30].

> **EFFET DE COMPLAISANCE**, *également appelé lettre, billet, papier ou traite de complaisance* [31],
>
> **LETTRE DE COMPLAISANCE**, *lettre de change endossée par un tiers de bonne réputation (appelé « complaisant ») qui agit comme garant accordant une faveur, sans rémunération aucune. La lettre de*

---

[30] William Krehm. A Power Unto Itself. Page 41, selon les estimations de Neil Brooks, fiscaliste de la Osgoode Hall Law School, le gouvernement perd huit milliards de dollars en revenus chaque année à cause d'abris fiscaux douteux.
[31] R. W. Jones, Thomson's Dictionary of Banking, New Era Publishing WINDBILLS, WINDMILLS, page 656 [TRADUCTION].

change peut être endossée en s'appuyant sur la solidité financière du garant qui demeure responsable jusqu'à ce qu'on ait acquitté la lettre de change [l'impôt à payer] [32],

TRAITE EN L'AIR OU EFFET CREUX, *« effet de complaisance » qui porte aussi le nom de « traite de complaisance »; les personnes qui tirent, acceptent ou endossent ces traites sont les « complaisants » ou « tirés »* [33].

Le président Trump, qui a obtenu des crédits d'impôt d'un milliard de dollars pour échapper à l'impôt fédéral pendant près de vingt ans, a déclaré :

« *La richesse de notre classe moyenne lui a été volée dans ses foyers pour être redistribuée partout dans le monde* [34]. » [TRADUCTION]

La présente analyse des effets de complaisance se fonde sur le rapport de 2009 commandé par le gouvernement du Canada qui a pour titre ABCP – Crisis in Canada et qui a été rédigé par le professeur John Chant, de l'Université Simon Fraser [35]. Le professeur Chant y définit le modèle d'affaires, d'une valeur de 112 milliards de dollars de PPAC, qui consistait à « acquérir pour distribuer » et qui est à l'origine de la plus grande faillite (32 milliards de dollars) d'un canalisateur financier dans l'histoire du Canada, au cours de la crise mondiale du crédit de 2008. Au sujet des centaines de milliards de dollars d'impôts non perçus par les autorités fiscales dans le monde, voici ce qu'a dit le professeur Larry Summers, président de l'Université Harvard et ancien secrétaire du Trésor, dans son discours de 2014 à la conférence du Toronto Institute of New Economic Thinking – INET portant sur le côté sombre de la mobilité du capital :

---

[32] Business Dictionary, http://www.businessdictionary.com/definition/accommodation-bill.html [TRADUCTION].
[33] Pitmans' Bills, Cheques, and Notes, 1907. Accommodation Bills, fictitious bills, page 28 [TRADUCTION].
[34] ABC 15 Arizona News, www.youtube.com/watch?v=Irrd10JjkBA.
[35] Étude du gouvernement du Canada sur le PPAC – la plus importante faillite de 32 milliards de dollars d'un canalisateur financier de l'histoire canadienne, le papier commercial adossé à des actifs, réalisée par le professeur John Chant de l'Université Simon Fraser de la C.-B. pour le groupe d'experts chargé d'examiner la réglementation des valeurs mobilières.

PROFESSEUR LARRY SUMMERS : « *Le journaliste américain Mike Kinsley a avancé la doctrine selon laquelle d'ordinaire, le vrai scandale ne réside pas dans les actes illégaux des gens, mais dans ce qui est pleinement légal. Et cela se vérifie certainement en ce qui a trait aux abris fiscaux, aux abris fiscaux outremer et aux abris fiscaux fournis par les institutions financières. Les abris fiscaux, l'arbitrage fiscal prennent des formes qui défient l'imagination. Mais, essentiellement, vous empruntez de l'argent, vous déduisez l'intérêt de vos emprunts et vous placez l'argent quelque part où des intérêts sont produits, mais vous ne payez pas d'impôt sur les intérêts perçus. Et si vous faites ces deux choses au même taux et que vous pouvez soustraire, vous vous rendez compte que vous faites un profit qui correspond au taux d'imposition multiplié par le taux d'intérêt sur chaque dollar de votre argent. Et il ne fait aucun doute que cela se produit couramment. Il ne fait aucun doute que sans ces activités lucratives de maximisation de la rente dans chaque pays, individuellement, cela se produirait beaucoup moins souvent. Il ne fait aucun doute que pour corriger pleinement ce problème, il faudrait que le niveau de coopération internationale dépasse celui que nous avons actuellement. Et il ne fait aucun doute que ce problème constitue un défi de taille, comme j'ai tâché de l'expliquer en parlant du côté sombre de la mobilité du capital. Je ne doute pas une seconde que des dizaines, voire des centaines, de milliards de dollars qui devraient être perçus par les autorités fiscales partout dans le monde* [36] *ne le sont pas, à cause de ces types d'activités d'arbitrage fiscal que vous décrivez* [37]*.* » [TRADUCTION]

La question des centaines de milliards de pertes de recettes monétisées pour des espèces sonnantes au moyen du régime fiscal a été présentée comme un miracle financier à ceux qui profitent de la perte en capital liée au revenu locatif déductible.

Prof Tyson : « *Il y a de l'argent en jeu. Dans l'optique des affaires, pourquoi les avocats, les comptables et les banquiers ne devraient-ils*

---

[36] Référence du dictionnaire : Fisc – n pl.–s a state or royal treasury [le trésor d'un État ou le trésor royal]. Réf : Dictionnaire Webster. Fiscal adj. of or pertaining to the public treasury or revenue [qui se rapporte au trésor public ou aux revenus de l'État] : Réf. : Collin's. Remarque : (Écosse) Fiscal n. treasurer, one who prosecutes for the Crown minor criminal cases. [Trésorier, personne qui poursuit en justice pour la Couronne dans les cas criminels de moindre importance].

[37] INET/CIGI Toronto Human After All Conference, avril 2014. Larry Summers aborde la question de la « stagnation séculaire », 12 avril 2014.

pas s'efforcer de faire de l'argent? Les contribuables étaient autorisés à déduire les pertes de placements passifs, comme des sociétés en commandite, pour contrebalancer de gros montants de revenu ordinaire d'autres sources. Au moyen de l'amortissement, les investisseurs pouvaient faire valoir des pertes sur des investissements qui, en fait, ont produit des bénéfices. Le modèle de base suppose l'utilisation de sociétés en commandite qui ont investi dans les biens tels que des ensembles d'habitations. Le revenu locatif serait plus que compensé par les dépenses d'exploitation, l'intérêt sur le prêt et l'amortissement, créant une perte que les partenaires pourraient utiliser pour éliminer l'impôt sur des dizaines de milliers de dollars de revenu d'autres sources. Au bout de cinq ans, l'ensemble d'habitations serait vendu à profit. Voilà ce que j'avais l'habitude d'appeler un miracle [38]. » [TRADUCTION]

Aux États-Unis, le sous-comité permanent sénatorial des enquêtes a remis en question la légalité des stratagèmes d'arbitrage fiscal de maximisation de la rente en 2005, décrits comme suit:

«Les sociétés en commandite ont investi dans des biens comme des ensembles d'habitations. Le revenu locatif serait largement compensé par les dépenses d'exploitation, l'intérêt sur le prêt et l'amortissement, créant une perte que les partenaires pourraient utiliser pour éliminer l'impôt sur des dizaines de milliers de dollars de revenu d'autres sources. Au bout de cinq ans, l'ensemble d'habitations serait vendu à profit.

«La frontière entre les abris appropriés ou non est tellement brouillée que l'IRS utilise des mots comme 'abusif' pour décrire les abris inacceptables au lieu de parler d'abris 'illégaux'. Mais dans une étude de 2005, le sous-comité permanent du Sénat des États-Unis a décrit les abris abusifs comme des 'opérations dont un des objectifs importants est l'évitement ou l'évasion fiscale concernant les impôts fédéraux, de l'État ou municipaux, d'une façon qui n'était pas prévue par la loi' [39]. » [TRADUCTION]

MAXIMISATION DE LA RENTE *n. Le fait d'essayer d'améliorer son revenu personnel aux dépens du revenu d'une autre personne, au lieu d'augmenter le travail ou la productivité. Certains économistes*

---

[38] Knowledge@Wharton, Tax Shelters: Exotic or Just Plain Illegal? Miracle Workers, page 2,
[39] http://knowledge.wharton.upenn.edu/article.cfm?articleid=1419 Tax Shelters: Exotic or Just Plain Illegal? Miracle Workers.

utilisent cette expres-sion pour décrire les processus au moyen desquels des personnes et des sociétés tentent d'utiliser le gouvernement pour promouvoir leurs propres intérêts, en particulier pour acquérir des sources de revenus (rentes) [40].

ARBITRAGE FISCAL : *Échanges de valeurs qui permet de profiter d'une différence entre les taux d'imposition ou les systèmes d'imposition comme base de profit*[41].

ARBITRAGE n. *(commerce) : Achat de biens à un endroit pour les vendre aussitôt ailleurs à un prix plus élevé; achat de lettres de change ou de titres et d'actions dans le même but* [42].

Au Canada, le coût de l'argent lié aux crédits d'impôt a fait l'objet d'une contestation devant la Cour fédérale du Canada en 2011 et celle-ci s'est prononcée contre la tenue d'un procès concernant le coût de l'argent associé à des crédits d'impôt douteux, estimé à mille milliards de dollars. La décision remet en question la sagesse du Parlement d'utiliser le taux interbancaire offert à Londres (LIBOR) pour des prêts bancaires outremer afin de frapper monnaie dans le territoire national au lieu de recourir au coût de l'argent à peu près nul de la Banque du Canada pour les crédits d'impôt sur le revenu gagné [43], et la Cour renvoie les contribuables devant le Parlement pour amorcer un débat public sur la politique gouvernementale.

Le vérificateur général du Canada est le comptable qui vérifie les livres du gouvernement. Dans son rapport annuel de 1993, il a reconnu que le plus gros de la dette du gouvernement consistait en frais d'intérêts. Ainsi, en 1993, la dette était composée à 91 % de frais d'intérêt, le gouvernement avait une dette de seulement 37 milliards de dollars canadiens (37 000 000 000 $) – très faible et soutenable, comme c'était aussi le cas avant 1974. Dès 2012, le gouvernement avait payé mille milliards de dollars canadiens (1 000 000 000 000) en intérêts – deux fois sa dette nationale [...] [44]

---

[40] Dictionary Central, http://www.dictionarycentral.com/definition/rent-seeking.html [TRADUCTION].
[41] The Free Dictionary, TAX ARBITRAGE, http://financial-dictionary.thefreedictionary.com/Tax+Arbitrage [TRADUCTION].
[42] Webster's Dictionary, édition encyclopédique de 1988. ARBITRAGE, page 47 [TRADUCTION].
[43] William Krehm c. La Banque du Canada. Cour fédérale du Canada, dossier T-2010-11.
[44] Ellen Brown, The Public Bank Solution. Third Millennium Press, 2013, Gross Canadian Federal Government debt 18672008. « From Sustainable to Unsustainable Debt », page 207.

Plus le coût de l'argent lié au taux d'intérêt était faible avant le krach de 2008 – plus l'impact du moins perçu en revenu lié aux crédits d'impôt sur le revenu était faible. L'arbitrage fiscal de maximisation de la rente au Canada aurait été moins profitable que les taux d'intérêt truqués du LIBOR qui maximisaient les rendements, comme suit :

LIBOR – *(London Inter-Bank Offered Rate) Taux interbancaire offert à Londres : taux d'intérêt moyen estimé par les principales banques à Londres qu'on leur imposerait pour un emprunt auprès d'autres banques. Le LIBOR est largement utilisé comme taux de référence pour de nombreux instruments financiers tant dans les marchés financiers que dans les secteurs commerciaux partout dans le monde. En juin 2012, de multiples ententes de règlement par la banque Barclays dans des causes criminelles ont révélé l'étendue de la fraude et de la collusion entre les banques membres, relativement à la présentation des taux, ce qui a mené au scandale du LIBOR* [45].

La cause que j'expose et que j'ai appelée l'échappatoire de la Magna Carta face aux tribunaux se fonde sur le principe d'« aucune taxation sans représentation » de 1215, principe sur lequel s'est fondée en 1694 la Banque d'Angleterre pour appliquer la politique gouvernementale et imprimer de l'argent capitalisé à partir de la valeur nette constituée des contribuables, puis en intégrant au service le coût de l'argent de la dette nationale liée aux crédits d'impôt; cette politique est à l'origine de la première économie déficitaire dans le monde qui fait appel à des banques privées.

Le plan du système bancaire médiéval a remplacé le bâton de comptage qui tenait lieu de devise sans intérêt pour la comptabilisation de l'impôt payé, par l'impôt en fiducie à prélever pour des banques privées ayant signé des promesses de verser des pièces d'une livre sur présentation de billets d'une livre et imposant le coût public de l'argent de l'intérêt de la rente sur les factures d'impôt impayées, au moyen de lettres de change comme monnaie légale.

Les promesses signées de verser de l'argent sur présentation de billets de la Banque d'Angleterre ont circulé dans les flux de trésorerie bancaires à l'échelle du pays qui monnayait des mouvements de capitaux de l'encaisse fractionnaire de la norme « or », au moyen du système bancaire et des sources de revenus dans les comptes budgétaires des impôts. Même aujourd'hui, on annonce, dans les discours du trône des

---

[45] Ellen Brown, The Public Bank Solution. Third Millennium Press, 2013, glossaire. LIBOR, page 433 [TRADUCTION].

gouvernements, des mesures budgétaires issues de promesses électorales après intégration de l'impôt dans la richesse publique et après émission d'« obligations » prenant appui sur des factures d'impôt impayées qui se retrouvent dans les flux de trésorerie d'économies déficitaires.

Selon le principe d'économie collective réelle, toute banque centrale détient un lien social sur la valeur fiscale reçue de la dette nationale; il en va autrement des effets de complaisance d'un système bancaire parallèle, qui constituent des liens spirituels sur la valeur théorique non reçue d'une dette conçue de façon trompeuse pour hausser le crédit en s'appuyant sur la contrefaçon.

Les effets de complaisance arrimés à des crédits d'impôt garnissent les déductions fiscales des contribuables crédules, qui monétisent l'intérêt fixé sur les effets de complaisance frauduleusement recyclés et blanchis, en raison des manques à gagner résultant de l'évitement fiscal et dissimulant des pertes, pour le Trésor national, qui sont intégrées dans la dette publique, mais qui ne sont pas inscrites au budget. Les effets de complaisance déductibles du revenu imposable produisent de l'intérêt jusqu'à ce que leurs « fabricants » endettés remboursent le principal dû bien que rien ne soit reçu et que les « titulaires » des effets de complaisance présentent à nouveau des promesses signées en vue de se faire payer à nouveau la dette théorique privée, cette fois inscrite comme dette nationale publique provenant de pertes imputées au Trésor.

Dans mon dossier T007385 portant sur les crédits d'impôt sur une hypothèque de cinq millions de dollars d'une propriété vendue comme s'il s'agissait d'un investissement, je suis devenu un partenaire dans une affaire permettant d'épargner au moyen de crédits d'impôt personnels dans un stratagème d'une valeur de plusieurs milliards de dollars. La commission secrète a préalablement accordé un prêt bancaire à l'extérieur du site, la clôture des prêts a lancé les flux de trésorerie d'épargne basée sur des crédits d'impôt, facturés par une banque comme s'il s'agissait de factures du partenariat hypothécaire sur lesquels j'ai payé l'intérêt du LIBOR, sur les manques à gagner des recettes fiscales par rapport à près de quinze millions ne figurant pas dans le budget sur la période de la rente de dix ans grevée par l'hypothèque. La rétention de la rente a provoqué le défaut de paiement de l'hypothèque assorti de ses effets de complaisance reposant sur un swap sur défaillance par défaut. Le fait de ne pas renouveler l'hypothèque grevée d'une rente de cinq millions de dollars a donné lieu à une procédure de recouvrement des effets de complaisance signés par la personne qui voulait faire des économies d'impôt, déjà remboursés une première fois par défaut dans un projet de « ventes-rachats » d'une propriété du FPI d'une valeur de dix millions de dollars, que la banque a facturée à nouveau pour la revente sur les marchés financiers tout en recouvrant les billets de demande de crédit bancaire signés par l'épargnant, par défaut, ainsi que les effets de complaisance de cet épargnant, et on a intenté des poursuites parce que le contribuable a accepté de rembourser un autre montant de cinq millions de dollars en argent comptant [...] ce qui représente le problème de conversion des effets de complaisance pour crédit d'impôt remboursé deux fois.

Ni la Magna Carta de 1215 ni la Loi sur les lettres de change de 1882 ne définissent de mesures législatives sur le contrôle des banques, et en 2016, la Cour fédérale du Canada a jugé irrecevable la cause d'arbitrage fiscal au sujet du fait que le gouvernement continue d'accorder des crédits d'impôt à des institutions financières qui profitent de désastres financiers et d'une dette nationale théorique. ÉCHAPPATOIRE

> **FISCALE, ÉCHAPPATOIRE** : *ambiguïté, omission ou exception (par exemple dans une loi ou un document légal) qui permet de se soustraire à l'application d'une règle sans en violer les exigences explicites; il s'agit plus particulièrement d'une disposition du code fiscal qui permet à un contribuable d'éviter de payer l'impôt sur le revenu ou d'en réduire le montant*xvii [46].

Dans tout ce que j'ai décrit ci-dessus, j'ai fait une déclaration sous serment sur la fraude fiscale, en soutenant que l'absence de contrôle des transactions bancaires constitue une échappatoire fiscale, faute d'une loi sur les contribuables crédules :

> ***Tout contribuable peut signer une promesse de payer de l'argent en contrepartie de dollars privés fictifs issus de crédits d'impôt fondés sur un effet de complaisance, que le Trésor pourra reconvertir sous forme de dette publique nationale fictive qu'il renverra à son « titulaire » en temps voulu.***

J'ai envoyé une présentation PowerPoint à mon député pour lui dire que je réclame toujours un projet de loi d'initiative parlementaire pour l'adoption d'une loi sur les contribuables crédules, pour que des mesures de contrôle des opérations bancaires protègent les consommateurs de biens financiers contre les effets de complaisance liés aux crédits d'impôt payés deux fois.

---

[46] Black's Law Dictionary, neuvième édition, LOOPHOLE, page 1028 [TRADUCTION].

28. Magna Carta Loophole ABCNotes of Law

Ruly English is chartered in the following Rule-of-Three socioeconomic prototype ABCNotes of law;

Step Transaction One: Tax Credit Windbill Sales Bank Balances of Accounts..................

Bills of Exchange Act, 1882 Accommodation Paper Windbill Maker Holder and Presentment Rules of Law
Revenue Canada Tax Credit Tax Shelter TS007385 / Tax Saver / Taxpayer SIN - Social Insurance Number
Tax Saver Accommodation Party Unreal Tax Credit Value Windbill Conversion to Money through Taxation
Rent Encumbered Mortgage on Income Producing Real Estate sold as Tax Shelter Investment in Property
Bank Agent Tax Shelter Broker Property Owner Unit Cost Bank Authorized Off-site Loans Closings
LIBOR - London Interbank Offered Rate Bank Technology CCAP - Central Credit Approval Process
Accounting Firm CA / Works of Arts Appraiser / Unlicensed Securities Dealer / Shadow Bank Sales Rep
Bank Agent Tax Shelter Broker: ❶Subscription Agreement, ❷Mortgage Note ❷CDS - Credit Default Swap,
❸Tax ❸Statement of Affairs, ❹Loan Note, ❺Agency Waiver, and ❻Affidavit of Subscribing Witness

B. Regulation by the Rule - Front Office Tax Shelter Deals
Accounting Firm CA as Unlicensed Securities Dealer Sells Tax Avoidance Scheme to Trusting Client
Tax Saver Signs Blank Tax Shelter Package including Mortgage Derivative and Loan Notes ❶❷❸❹❺❻
CA Inflates Tax Saver ❸Tax ❸Statement of Affairs that the Taxpayer Appears Tax Creditworthy
CA Signs ❻Affidavit of Subscribing Witness that Tax Saver on ❷Mortgage Note is Taxpayer on ❹Loan Note

C. Enforcement of the Rule - Front Office Bank Agent Tax Shelter Broker Tied Loan Sales
Tax Shelter Broker as Lawyer checks ❶❷❸❹❺❻ and Inchoate ❹Loan Note is Signed but not Dated
Bank Agent Broker Notarizes CA ❻Affidavit of Subscribing Witness as signed by Shadow Bank Sales Rep
Bank Agent Broker Commissions ❸Tax ❸Statement of Affairs as per Tax Saver ❶Subscription Agreement

C. Enforcement of the Rule - Back Office New Bank Client Tax Credit Savings Loan Accounts
Check ❺Agency Waiver, ❻Affidavit of Subscribing Witness signed same date as ❷Mortgage Note
Bank Inflates Net Worth of ❸Tax ❸Statement of Affairs that the Taxpayer Appears Personal Creditworthy
Bank Rebrands Blank ❹Loan Note with *Rubberstamp* Logo and written Branch Name and Address
New Client Record with CA ❻Affidavit of Subscribing Witness dual signed Shadow Bank Loan Sales Rep
Bank copied Taxpayer Private Information for 1x Unit Cost PLSA - Personal Loan Service Application

A. ABCNotes of Law - Bank Tied Loan Tax Shelter Sales Pending Credit Approvals
CCAP History Flags 9 Credit Alerts due to Taxpayer Debt and Unpaid Business and Personal Credit Cards

B. Regulation by the Rule - Back Office Bank Tax Credit Loan Decisions
Bank Adjudicates Taxpayer Net Worth and Income as Tax Saver to Carry LIBOR Cost of Money to Invest
Bank Lending Decision Bank Agent Tax Shelter Broker Consigns Tax Saver Tax Credits to same Taxpayer
Bank Decision to Shadow Bank Loan Sales Rep to fill out ❹Loan Note Amount for CA to Close a Sale

B. Regulation by the Rule - Front Office Tax Shelter Sales Management
CA Upsells Tax Shelter Units Sold and Bank Agent Tax Shelter Broker Doubles 2x Tied Loan Amount
CA Written ❹Loan Note at 2x Unit Cost and Prime + 1% Changed to ~~Prime~~ + 1% with Tax Saver Initials
Bank Agent Tax Shelter Broker Returned ❹Loan Note for the Bank to Date in Off-site Loans Closings

A. ABCNotes of Law – Bank Head Office Collateral Deficiency Notifications
Audit Report Taxpayer $100,000 Mortgage and ❹Loan Note Changed and Initialed in Different Color Inks
Audit Advises Bank Contact Tax Saver to Sign New ❹Loan Note for Tax Shelter Broker to Process the Loan

B. Regulation by the Rule – Back Office Bank Management of Tax Credit Loans
Bank Writes Memo Bank Agent Tax Shelter Broker Need Not Contact Tax Saver to Sign New ❹Loan Note
Bank Dates ❹Loan Note Passed Through Bank Agent Tax Shelter Broker Off-site Loans Closings

B. Regulation by the Rule – Front Office Off-site Loans Closings Tax Shelter Sales
CA Fills Out Bank Loan Dependent Unit Cost Quantities on ❷Mortgage Note and Signs as Bank Paid Witness
Bank Agent Tax Shelter Broker Signs ❷Mortgage Note in Acceptance of Tax Credit Value is Money Whereof

C. Enforcement of the Rule – Back Office Bank CCAP System Filed Loan Documents
Bank CCAP Updates Tax Saver Closings and Taxpayer Account Setup Screens for Unacknowledged Loan
Bank Files ❸Statement of Affairs, ❹Loan Note, ❺Agency Waiver, and ❻Affidavit of Subscribing Witness
Bank Issues Cheque from Total Proceeds of all ❹Loan Note to Bank Agent Tax Shelter Broker

A. ABCNotes of Law – Front Office Tax Shelter Syndication Deals Sold
Broker Settles CA Secret Commission from Bank Loans that CA Witnessed Taxpayer Sign ❹Loan Note
CA Delivers Taxpayer Tax Shelter ❶Subscription Agreement and ❷Mortgage Note Deal to Tax Saver
Bank Agent Tax Shelter Broker Discounts Total Tax Shelter ❷Mortgage Note Tax Credit Value Received

A. ABCNotes of Law – Back Office Tax-Credit Savings Loan Account Setup
Bank Letter of Introduction from Bank to Tax Saver Confirming Purchase Price of 1 Unit of Tax Shelter
Bank Bills Taxpayer 12 Month Tax Saver Interest Cost of Tax Credit to an Unnumbered Bank Account

Step Transaction Two: Tax Credit Windbill Interest Bank Balances of Accounts...................

A. Triune System Rule of Law – Rent Seeking Mortgage Derivative Tax Credit Interest Revenue Shortfall
Tax Credit Accommodation Paper Signed by a Tax Saver Maker is Taxpayer Secured Money to its Holder

B. Regulation by the Rule – Front Office Bank Agent Tax Shelter Rent Paid Mortgage on Account
Bank Agent Tax Shelter Broker Collects Property Rent Paid as Interest Underlying Mortgage Account

B. Regulation by the Rule – Back Office Bank Mortgage Partnership Tax Credit Savings Loan Account
Bank Invoice to Taxpayer to Deposit Tax Credit Mortgage Partnership Interest Charges Billed on Account
Tax Saver Remits Bank Invoiced Mortgage Derived Interest Payments to Invest Tax Credit Savings

C. Enforcement of the Rule – Back Office Tax Shelter TS007385 Financial Conduit in Bank Profits
Bank Posts Tax Saver Bank Prime +1% Monthly Deposits to Tax Shelter Invoice Payments Account

A. ABCNotes of Law – Company Business Owner and Personal Income Tax Returns
Accounting Firm CA Prepares Company Books, Unlicensed Securities Dealer Prepares Income Tax Returns

B. Regulation by the Rule – Accounting Firm Bookkeeping for the Taxpayer Tax Credit Saver
Bank Unnumbered Invoice Payments Account Confirmation of Interest Charges on 2 Units of Tax Shelter
Unlicensed Securities Dealer Fills out Tax Shelter Rent Loss Schedule for Personal Income Tax Credit
CA Calculates Shareholder Account to Increase Taxpayer Income from the Company Owner in Business

C. Enforcement of the Rule – Taxpayer Company Business and Personal Income Tax Statements
CA for Taxpayer and Tax Saver Files Company Business and Personal Income Tax Returns

A. ABCNotes of Law – Canada Revenue Agency Audit
CA for the Taxpayer Prepares for CRA Audit of Company Business and Personal Income Tax Returns

B. Regulation by the Rule – Canada Revenue Agency Audit to Reassess Income Tax Credit Bill
CRA Bills Personal Tax Reassessment and Shareholders Ordered to Pay Income Tax Deductions on Payroll

C. Enforcement of the Rule – Taxpayer Restructured Business Consistent with Tax Policy
Company Owners on Payroll with all Work Outsourced to Temporary Hires and Suppliers as Needed

Step Transaction Three: Tax Credit Windbill Principal Bank Balances of Accounts..................

A. Triune System Rule of Law – Rent Seeking Tax Credit Mortgage Derivative Principal Liability
Bank Agent Tax Shelter Broker Collects Mortgage Tax Credit Value Windbill on Tax Saver Account

B. Regulation by the Rule – Front Office Tax Shelter Mortgage Failure to Rollover in Default
Taxpayer Paid Interest on Bank Agent Tax Shelter Broker Property Rent Paid Mortgage over 10 Year Term
Tax Shelter Broker Managing Partner Announced Mortgagor Refusal to Remortgage Property in Receivership
Managing Partner Votes to Sell the Property without Disclosing Ownership as DIP – Debtor in Possession
Tax Shelter Broker Collects ❷Mortgage Note ❷CDS – Credit Default Swap that Pays for the Property Sale
Tax Saver Repays Underlying Mortgage the Tax Shelter Broker Reacquired Own Property Mortgage Free
Tax Shelter Broker Does Not Cancel ❷Mortgage Note and Dissolves the Partnership in Final Disbursements
Property Resold as REIT – Real Estate Investment Trust that the Broker Manages in Bank Capital Markets

Step Transaction Four: Tax Credit Windbill Contingent Liability Bank Balances of Accounts..................

A. Triune System Rule of Law – Off-Book Unnumbered Tax Credit Savings Loan Contingent Liability
Bank Collects Off-the-books Mortgage Derivative Contingent Liability in Taxpayer Tax Saver Signed Name
ABCP – Asset Backed Commercial Paper Post 2008 Credit Crunch 2009 ABCP *'Crisis in Canada'* Report
Court Settlement of the Largest $32billion Bankruptcy of a Financial Conduit in Canadian History
COMER – Committee on Monetary and Economic Reform Action against Bank of Canada and Budget Process

B. Regulation by the Rule – Back Office Bank Tax Credit Savings Loan Account
Bank Presents Photocopy of Mortgage Partnership ❹Loan Note to Taxpayer to Repay Tax Shelter Loan
Tax Saver Discovers Misleading Loan and Alleges Securities Fraud in Defense
Bank Claim Relies on ❸Statement of Affairs, ❺Agency Waiver, and ❻Affidavit of Subscribing Witness

B. Regulation by the Rule – Tax Shelter TS007385 Finance, Law, Economics Prototype Gap Analysis
Tax Saver JAD *'Signature Specific Identity Theft'* Bank ❹Loan Note Dependent Tax Shelter Dataflow
Taxpayer Defines Bank System JAD Business Model that Lawyers Edit with Bank Terminology
Taxpayer Reports CA to ICAO and Alleged Securities Fraud to Police in Case of Criminal Acts

C. Enforcement of the Rule – Bank Action Civil Court Files
Taxpayer Deposits Discoveries including Tax Shelter Mortgage Deeds and Rent Assignments in Court File

A. ABCNotes of Law – Court Rules Debt without Trial and Deny Appeals for Trial
Bank Sues Photocopy of Mortgage Partnership ❹Loan Note to Collect Tax Credit Loan Savings Account
Lawyer for Taxpayer Files Bank Agent Tax Shelter Broker Noted in Default to Defend to Different Court

B. Regulation by the Rule – Court Collects Photocopy of Seemingly Forged Note for the Bank
Lawyer for Tax Saver Abandons Case that Taxpayer Pleads for Trial of Tax Credit ❷Mortgage Note
Lawyer for Bank Denies ❷Mortgage Note Exists and Judge Rules Summary Judgment for the Bank

B. Regulation by the Rule – Bank Lien for Court Ordered Debt
Lawyer for Bank Refuses to Clear Bank Lien on Taxpayer Residence until Release Signed for all Parties
Lawyer for Bank Refuses to Cancel and Return ❹ Loan Note to Taxpayer as Signed by the Tax Saver

C. Enforcement of the Rule – Final Settlement of Bank Claimed Debt and Legal Fees
Taxpayer Certified Cheque Deposit to Bank Court Ordered Debt and Cash Paid Money to Bank Lawyer

A. ABCNotes of Law – Canada Revenue Agency Correspondence
Lawyer for Taxpayer Oversees Bank Remove Lien with Claims, Counter-claims and Cross-claims Releases

B. Regulation by the Rule – Pan Canadian Investors Committee
$32 billion illiquid ABCP Third Party Notes Subprime Mortgage Failures to Rollover in $117billion Market
ABCP Bankrupt Bank Bailout Claims for Payments of Unpaid CDO – Collateralized Debt Obligations
Double Presentments of ❷ Mortgage Note ❷ CDS – Credit Default Swap ABCP Financial Instruments

C. Enforcement of the Rule – 2008 Montreal Accord ABCP Restructuring Plan
Court Order for Investor Committee Protection under CCAA – Companies' Creditors Arrangement Act
Comprehensive Release of US$1million Class of ABCP Third Parties for both Negligence and Fraud
ABCP Conduit Commercial Paper converted to MAV – Master Asset Vehicles and Tracking Notes.

A. ABCNotes of Law – Court Order to Recapitalize ABCP Third Party Notes
Tax Saver Paid Windbill on Private Account Repaid in Same Name of Taxpayer SIN on Public Account

B. Regulation by the Rule – 2011 COMER Lawsuit for Trial of Bank of Canada and Federal Budget Process
Lawyer for COMER Argument that Offshore Bank Loans for Onshore Money is a Breach of Constitution
COMER Argument Budget Process Violates Magna Carta *'No Taxation without Representation'* Principle
Taxpayer and Expert Witness COMER Files Request for Court Appointed Assessor of Economic Impact

C. Enforcement of the Rule – Supreme Court of Canada Correspondence with Interested Taxpayer
Refused to Accept Evidence of Magna Carta Loophole Twice Paid Tax Credit Windbill Conversions

A. Triune System of Law – 2017 Supreme Court of Canada Endorses 2014 Federal Court Ruling
Federal Court T-20 0-11 Justice Russell Advice that Taxpayers should complain to their representatives

NB: ABCNotes™ © Anthony Crawford 2019 is a Proprietary Software APP used to translate Ruly English words of law to compile a system technology design in pseudo code.

www.ingramcontent.com/pod-product-compliance
Lightning Source LLC
Chambersburg PA
CBHW031926240526
45464CB00023B/1684